## Praise for *Lost Soul, Wise Soul*

"Brilliant! Provocative! Groundbreaking! Expands the work of Michael Newton and deepens our understanding of the purpose of our lives. *Lost Soul, Wise Soul* shows us both the pull towards darkness and the pathway to liberation. A master therapist, Karen Joy's selection of cases demonstrates the debilitating struggle some souls endure before reemergence in the light. Regardless of the detour, length of delay, or perceived disconnection, souls eventually awaken to their inherent connection to Source. I recommend this book for anyone struggling to find their way out of darkness or their own abiding connection to Source."

—Joanne Selinske, Cht, PhD, Michael Newton Institute
practitioner and author of *Awakened Soul*

# LOST
# SOUL

## HOW CHALLENGING PAST LIVES
## SHAPE OUR FUTURE

# WISE
# SOUL

## KAREN JOY

# About the Author

Karen Joy was a psychologist in private practice for over twenty years before shifting her focus to conducting regressions into past lives and life between lives. Trained by the Newton Institute for Life Between Lives Hypnotherapy, she felt called to share the life-changing regressions of her clients. *Lost Soul, Wise Soul* is her fourth book on regressions after *Other Lives, Other Realms: Journeys of Transformation*, *Llewellyn's Little Book of Life Between Lives* (coauthor), and *Wisdom of Souls: Case Studies of Life Between Lives from the Michael Newton Institute* (coauthor).

Karen is happily married to Ian Demack, author and writing coach, and lives in the beautiful village of Maleny in the hinterland of the Sunshine Coast in Australia. Between them, they have three children, five grandchildren, and two great grandchildren.

Karen's website is https://lifebetweenlivesregression.com.au.

# LOST SOUL

## SOUL

### HOW CHALLENGING PAST LIVES
### SHAPE OUR FUTURE

# WISE

# SOUL

## KAREN JOY

LLEWELLYN PUBLICATIONS
WOODBURY, MINNESOTA

FIRST EDITION
First Printing, 2022

Book design by Colleen McLaren
Cover design by Shannon McKuhen
Interior art by Llewellyn Art Department

Llewellyn Publications is a registered trademark of Llewellyn Worldwide Ltd.

**Library of Congress Cataloging-in-Publication Data**
Names: Joy, Karen, author.
Title: Lost soul, wise soul : how challenging past lives shape our future / Karen Joy.
Description: First edition. | Woodbury, Minnesota : Llewellyn Worldwide, Ltd, 2022. | Includes bibliographical references. | Summary: "Drawing on her most compelling client cases, author Karen Joy describes the natural arc of a soul's journey over many lifetimes–including violent or negative ones– until we finally come back to the light"-- Provided by publisher.
Identifiers: LCCN 2021049113 (print) | LCCN 2021049114 (ebook) | ISBN 9780738770079 | ISBN 9780738770215 (ebook)
Subjects: LCSH: Reincarnation.
Classification: LCC BL515 .J69 2022 (print) | LCC BL515 (ebook) | DDC 202/.37--dc23/eng/20211201
LC record available at https://lccn.loc.gov/2021049113
LC ebook record available at https://lccn.loc.gov/2021049114

Llewellyn Worldwide Ltd. does not participate in, endorse, or have any authority or responsibility concerning private business transactions between our authors and the public.

All mail addressed to the author is forwarded but the publisher cannot, unless specifically instructed by the author, give out an address or phone number.

Any internet references contained in this work are current at publication time, but the publisher cannot guarantee that a specific location will continue to be maintained. Please refer to the publisher's website for links to authors' websites and other sources.

Llewellyn Publications
A Division of Llewellyn Worldwide Ltd.
2143 Wooddale Drive
Woodbury, MN 55125-2989
www.llewellyn.com

Printed in the United States of America

# Other Books by Karen Joy

*Other Lives, Other Realms: Journeys of Transformation*

*Llewellyn's Little Book of Life Between Lives*
(with Ann J. Clark, Marilyn Hargreaves, and Joanne Selinske)

*Wisdom of Souls: Case Studies of Life Between Lives*
*from the Michael Newton Institute*
(with Ann J. Clark, Joanne Selinske, and Marilyn Hargreaves)

*What you disown in yourself*

*owns you.*

# Acknowledgments

There are many to thank. My deep gratitude to my clients who have taught me so much and made this book possible. My teachers are many, including colleagues and members of the Newton Institute for Life Between Lives Hypnotherapy. Thanks to all the skilled people at my publisher, Llewellyn Worldwide, who have backed the book and significantly improved it—in particular, Angela Wix for her advocacy and support, my copy editor, Hanna Grimson, and the great publicity team.

I am forever thankful to family members and friends who have been supportive and encouraging, including Colleen La Botz, Marina Mueller-nixon, Jane Teresa Anderson, Michael Collins, Erica Duguid, Tracy-Jayne Webb, Glenn Martin, Helena Wilson, Elizabeth Watson, Lisbeth Lysdale, and Rachel Hannam. Special thanks to those who read the draft manuscript and made helpful comments: Joanne Selinske, Lynn Parker, Ann Clark, Sally Douglas, and Liara Covert. The help of Jim Demack and Lionel Hogg is also appreciated. My eternal gratitude goes to the one who has taught me so much I wouldn't know where to begin, my writing mentor, husband, and love of my life, Ian Demack.

# Disclaimer

The material in this book is not intended as a substitute for trained medical or psychological advice. Readers are advised to consult their personal healthcare professionals regarding treatment. The publisher and the author assume no liability for any injuries caused to the reader that may result from the reader's use of the content contained herein.

# Contents

## SECTION 1: BEFORE THE FALL

## SECTION 2: INTO THE DEPTHS

## SECTION 3: ARISING

## SECTION 4: BUILDING BALANCE

# INTRODUCTION

Soon after I started conducting past life regressions, one of my former psychology clients came to see me. Yvette, an engineer, was an attractive young woman who'd recently broken up a short relationship. As a psychologist, I had helped her work through her childhood traumas several years earlier. Her parents had used her as a pawn during their tumultuous relationship, separation, and divorce. During our sessions, Yvette resolved the hurt she felt toward her mother and any anger directed at her father. She saw me regularly for over a year, and I came to admire her intelligence, courage, and honesty. Now, she wanted a past life regression.

This time her issue was completely different. She had made peace with her family and was happy with her life, apart from one recurring problem. "I'm attracted to narcissists," she blurted out. During the last twelve months, the three men with whom she'd become involved all turned out to be self-centered, arrogant, manipulative, and controlling.

Yvette's well-developed intuitive sense rarely let her down. She couldn't understand why she'd failed to discern the nature of these men sooner. In the beginning, she was strongly attracted to each of them. Only after several months of dating did she realize how demanding and critical they were.

After she has described her problem, Yvette settles back in her chair. I induct her into a trance state. As she goes in deeper, I ask why she gravitated toward such unsatisfactory relationships.

1

While she is lying in the chair with her eyes closed, I click my fingers to indicate that the information is now available. I ask her what is happening. Even before I finish my question, she exclaims loudly, *Oh my God! I am a man in a market. I am struggling to believe this, but I know it is true. I am selling people! I am a slave trader!*

I can see Yvette is disturbed so I suggest she take a few slow, deep breaths. She does, but her agitation soon takes over again. With a sense of outrage in her voice, she describes the scenes unfolding in her mind's eye.

*The people I am selling have been stolen! They are all light-skinned and standing here naked. Some of the slaves are children!*

Yvette sounds distressed by the slave trader's actions, so I ask how she feels. She pauses, looking thoughtful. From her shocked earlier reactions, I expect her to be dismayed. Instead, her voice deepens, and I hear a smug hardness in her reply.

*I feel proud of myself. I am making good money. There is a mean old man buying a young teenage girl. I am laughing, relishing the thought that she will suffer. She is looking at me in despair, and I am just enjoying it.*

This shocked me. I expected Yvette to condemn the slave trader, to show mercy or at least pity. Instead, she relished the inevitable suffering of the young slave girl in the hands of a lecherous old man. I struggled to make sense of her callous disdain. Where had it come from? How could someone as compassionate as Yvette—the woman her friends and family looked to for kindness and wisdom—suddenly turn so cold? How could such a cruel past life still have a hold over someone as lovely as Yvette?

## Souls Evolve. But How?

This session with Yvette began an obsession. I wanted to understand how caring people could still harbor aspects of malice deeply buried within them. To Yvette's horror, she found the callousness of the slave trader had not been washed away. She felt it during the regression, and it was affecting her life. Why did her attraction to narcissists have a hold on her in her current life? How did that attraction relate to the slave trader? What purpose, if any, did it serve? And why were these cruel tendencies buried in the first place? Was this by accident or by design?

In his books, Michael Newton claimed that we plan our lives. If we choose our lives, why would we choose to be evil? If we were evil in a life, could that affect our subsequent lives? And if it did, how did that happen?

Over the last two thousand years, philosophers and theologians have debated the nature of evil, but none from the perspective of past life and life between lives regressions. These spiritual regressions use hypnosis to access our past lives and our life between our lives. During a spiritual regression, we have a unique focus. We are able to burrow down into our deepest motivations and proclivities, dissecting their origin and progression, before tracking a path forward toward enlightenment. We receive the answers we desire as we trace the arc of our soul's incarnations on earth.

## Life Between Lives Hypnosis

Our life between lives, also known as the afterlife, has many dimensions and contains our spiritual home. We return there after death and can visit this place during a special hypnotic regression.

Accessing our deep unconscious memories is facilitated by this amazing process called *hypnosis*. In a hypnotic trance, people can shift their attention away from their current life circumstances to relive their past lives and visit their life between lives. This is not just an information-gathering exercise. Clients experience their past lives and life between lives subjectively through the prism of their current life. Having experienced this myself, I would describe it as receiving a download of information in thoughts, feelings, images, ideas, and impressions and then translating that experience into words, sometimes using current references to describe what is being received. Although clients access their past lives and life between lives with the knowledge and experience of their current self, this is not a "thinking" process. The information is *received*. I always ask for the first thing they get, as later thoughts can be the result of analyzing with the conscious mind.

I help clients attain a focused and receptive state of presence through hypnosis. In this relaxed and trusting state, their conscious thinking mind becomes the observer while a deeper part of the psyche is open to information that emerges into their calm, perceptive awareness. In the beginning, information usually surfaces in response to questions. As the client gains confidence, the information begins to flow easily, assisted by the client's intention for the session and his or her inherent curiosity.

During each session, I am a facilitator. The client's spiritual guides and higher self are in control, focusing the client's attention and delivering the information they need. I reflect my client's words back to them before asking clarifying questions. If my clients encounter any blocks, I use my skills, knowledge, and experience to help them confront, accept, and integrate these shadow aspects of themselves. The shadow includes characteristics, behaviors, and knowledge that we mentally disown and deny.

Throughout the regression, clients remain in a state of receptive awareness, meaning they are focused on being open and accepting of whatever they are receiving in the present moment. When they are immersed in a scenario set in another era and place where they identify as being a completely different person, we refer to this as a past life. When they are visiting nonphysical dimensions such as their soul group, wise elders, or repositories of information, we know this is the afterlife, the life between lives.

## Do Past Lives and the Afterlife Exist?

When people regress to a past life, are they really accessing a time when they lived previously? And when they move on to their life between lives, are they really visiting the afterlife?

There is no absolute way of knowing, but there is plenty of supporting evidence from many different sources if you go looking for it. In this book I am setting out what I have observed, heard, and experienced. I am in a most privileged position. I witness hundreds of people delving into the depths of their psyches. I feel obliged to write about the knowledge and wisdom I receive. It seems my clients share this sense too because they all willingly signed copyright releases so their words can be published.[1] I thank them humbly for their generosity.

In the regressions, clients have their own interpretation of what they encounter. They arrive at my office with a keen sense of curiosity. They either believe in past lives and life between lives or are open to the possibility. A few hope to receive proof of life after death. However, I don't recommend this as a useful focus.

To remember anything, we need to use our imagination. Our spiritual guides and higher selves utilize our imaging ability to conjure our past lives and life between lives.

Some people question what they are receiving, wondering if they are making it all up. Some fret that they are wasting their time or money. Their worries reflect their human vulnerability and self-doubt, but I ask them to put these concerns aside for the

---

1. Clients' names have been changed for privacy reasons.

5

time being. Moving into other realms means leaving the physical world and its fears behind. Undertaking a mental analysis during the regression blocks the receptive process.

Each person has to make up their own mind about the validity of their regression. I suggest my clients analyze what they receive later if they wish to test it for evidence. Like the clients, I have assumed the stories in this book are sufficiently real to be valuable, and I have treated them this way in order to glean the lessons they present.

I trust my clients. They are curious and seekers of truth. They want to make sense of their lives and find their purpose. Many of my clients are grounded people, including engineers, health professionals, tradesmen, IT technicians, scientists, administrators, lawyers, teachers, academics, managers, and business owners. Quite a few are retired. Some are healers and creatives. These clients come believing there is more than just their physical existence. They find that we are more than our physical body and more than the nonphysical spirit that inhabits our body. This spirit is part of our soul.

## The Earth System

Where does our spirit go after it leaves the body? Our emotions, attitudes, and identity emanate a unique frequency. At the moment of separation, the quality of our frequency determines where our spirit goes. Other authors report that our spirit rejoins our soul. Although this is often the case, it only happens when our spirit and soul are vibrationally matched.

Imagine earth being the center of concentric bands of vibrational energy. The frequencies close to the earth are lower, providing places for earthbound spirits who are confused, lost, or stuck. Michael Newton, a psychologist who conducted a great many past life and life between lives regressions, mentioned places of seclusion for certain dysfunctional souls. He found very few of these secluded souls in the thousands of clients he saw in his practice. Most of his clients, in their past lives, returned to their soul home after death.[2] I describe this as a place of higher and lighter vibrational energy. In this analogy, our soul home would be in the outer concentric bands. Here we find places of learning, which include schools, a council of wise elders, libraries, and soul relatives.

My clients found places where spirits can rest or be restored. These are the in-between levels of the life between lives, the mid-level frequency bands. Clients experiencing these vibrations were told they needed restoration before going home to higher levels or to rest before returning to a subsequent life on earth. The earth and these vibrational bands form what I call the earth system. At our physical death, our spirit is drawn to its vibrational match, which could be at any level in the nonphysical frequencies within the earth system.

Our soul usually occupies the higher levels of non-physicality that Michael Newton described. But souls, as well as spirits, can be stunted in their development, affecting the nature of their vibration. The level of our vibrational signature is a reflection of our choices, and this is explored in detail in the book.

Cyclic movement is part of the earth system. For example, our soul invests in physical form repeatedly—back and forth to birth and death on earth and then back to our life between lives.

## The Arc of Our Soul Journey

If we step back and take a large perspective—looking at the arc of our journey through our earthly incarnations—we see a pattern.

2. Michael Newton, *Destiny of Souls: New Case Studies of Life Between Lives* (St. Paul, MN: Llewellyn Publications, 2000), 104–105.

Our lighter lives are ordinary and pleasant with the usual challenges of life. But we also have lives of darker shades. At one or more times during many incarnations, we find ourselves at a pivotal point, approaching a crossroads with two choices: darkness or light. Which direction shall we now choose?

When we choose separation, perhaps becoming hapless victims or cold-hearted villains, we can take a long time to find our way back to connection. This is our dark night of the soul, a descent into isolating from Source and others. Even when we begin to awaken, we can struggle in our lives. We need to step up and learn to trust, connect, and open again to love. When we finally reach liberation, we have many resources at our disposal, such as renewed confidence, inner strength, gratitude, knowledge, compassion, and wisdom.

## Understanding the Darker Side of Human Existence

As you read on, you will discover the reason why souls choose a path of separation and its various iterations. You'll also learn why, in some lives, souls become lost. You will learn how souls emerge during a powerful pivotal life and the struggles they face on their way back to the light. Most importantly, you are given an understanding of this amazing earth system and the arc of our soul journey through it. You see the purpose of the dark night of the soul: the treasures souls reap from both their experiences of connection and their challenges of separation. You understand the fundamental value of contrast, which is an essential part of incarnating on this awesome planet.

This doesn't mean we can excuse ourselves for doing terrible things by saying it is just part of our soul journey. All of our actions have consequences. You will learn that suffering the ramifications of our actions is an important, yet painful, part of our soul journey.

There is much terror, corruption, and destruction in our world. Some of us have a dark fascination with those engaging in barbarous actions, while others turn away, preferring to avoid looking at the worst impulses of human nature. And yet most of us wonder why there is so much turmoil in our world and why some people are so ruthless. As you read through the cases in this book, you will have an opportunity to understand the hostile tendencies humans can express. My hope is that the stories will increase your understanding of our tumultuous world.

The cases in the book come from the courageous journeys of my clients, which I have vicariously experienced with them. I chose the cases carefully in the hope they would illuminate the purpose of challenging emotions such as loss, pain, isolation, and cruelty, while expanding concepts of love, joy, and appreciation.

Although I have done hundreds of regressions, I do not claim that the conclusions that I have drawn, nor the experiences explored in the regressions, are universal. I am sharing the wisdom I have gleaned from many sources, including regressions where the messages revealed significant consistency. However, it is wise to keep in mind that the information may not apply directly to you. I advise following your own spiritual guidance and coming to your own personal conclusions about what I present.

## Outline of the Book

Before we begin, you will find a segment called "Potentially Helpful Processes," which follows this introduction. You may find some of the cases in this book disturbing. If so, this segment contains some suggestions that you might find useful as you read through the book.

The book is divided into four sections. The first, "Before the Fall," explores our early incarnations on earth and how challenges take us astray. The first chapter, "Beginning the Journey," sets the scene by exploring the nature of a soul, the attraction of the earth system, and how we begin our incarnations and acclimatize to earth. The second, "Getting Lost," explains how we lose our way and why, demonstrating how past life energy can carry over and influence our current life like a still-active computer program running in the background.

Then we move to the next section, "Into the Depths," which has four chapters. The first three detail clients' journeys into lives of amoral or criminal actions. They are chapter 3, "Agreeing to Be the Perpetrator," chapter 4, "Descent into Assault and Torture," chapter 5, "The Dark Path of Vampirism and Domination." We explore the reason for each soul's descent into these challenging lives and their gradual emergence back into light. Chapter 6, "The Transition of Lost Souls," examines how souls, contaminated by their earthly lives, begin their journey back to light and how spiritual guides help them progress.

The next section, "Arising," shows us how souls develop the courage to open up both emotionally and spiritually. "Softening," chapter 7, assesses the benefits of suffering loss and pain and how one can melt frozen emotions. In chapter 8, "Emerging," we examine the current and past lives of two clients moving from separation and despair through confusion and vulnerability to greater strength and peace. Chapter 9, "Learning to Love," explores the different impediments to love experienced by three clients.

In the last section, "Building Balance," we meet souls refining necessary abilities and qualities as they move closer to the end of their incarnations on earth. In chapter 10, "Avoiding the Depths," we discover how some souls manage to bypass the perpetrator path in their earth incarnations. In chapter 11, "Inner Strength and Balance," we find a soul utilizing skill and wisdom to attain balance in practice. In chapter 12, "Spiritual Surrender," we examine the nature of surrender as we proceed toward the final stages of incarnation.

Our physical and emotional reactions are clues to our soul history. As you read the cases in this book, you might find some of them provoke a reaction within you. Perhaps you find a situation or character either repulsive or compelling. Aspects of the story may stay present in your mind. If this happens, I suggest you take note. Very likely, there is something related to the story that you could choose to explore. Taking time to investigate may give you more information about your true self and your past life experiences.

As we proceed through the book, we learn how souls begin their journey connected to Source, how they lose their connection, and eventually find it again. Through all our lifetimes of experience, we are developing our intuitive wisdom.

Our intuition grows wise over time. Guided by Source, we take on varied experiences, make countless decisions, reap the consequences, see the myriad connections between us all, and gradually gain an understanding of ourselves and our world. We emerge deeply connected to higher wisdom and spiritual truth, each of us living a unique, authentic life.

Now, let's begin our journey of discovery, learning what we take on when we decide to incarnate into the earth system and how we proceed through lifetimes of challenges until we finally reach a state where we radiate grace, trust, and wisdom.

# POTENTIALLY HELPFUL PROCESSES

This section has been designed as an option to help you if you feel disturbed while reading the book. Please be aware that these processes are *not* a substitute for professional treatment from doctors, psychologists, or other health professionals. By consulting a professional, you receive personal interactive guidance that keeps you safe.

## Calming Exercise

You can practice this simple exercise right now, knowing that the more you use it, the easier and more effective it becomes.

1. Take in a slow deep breath.
2. Hold it for a couple of seconds.
3. Now breathe out slowly.

Do that again, but this time pay attention to your bodily sensations.

1. Take in a slow deep breath, noticing how your chest and belly expand.
2. Hold the expansion for a couple of seconds.
3. Now breathe out slowly, noticing the sensation of release.

Repeat for a third time, bringing your imagination into play.

1. Slowly, take in a deep breath of fresh new air and energy, imagining that it is full of revitalizing oxygen and refreshing, sparkling cleansing light as it expands through you.

2. As you hold your breath for a couple of seconds, imagine the oxygen and light nurturing the cells of your body and relaxing your muscles.

3. Breathe out slowly, imagining a release of all negativity and heaviness, which flows outward from your body, disappearing into the distance. This can be a feeling of release, with a sense of energy draining out of your body.

4. Continue very slowly—you do not want to hyperventilate—until you feel calm.

You can use this process quietly and privately anytime you feel disturbed. It is a great technique to have as a resource. As soon as you are aware of any disturbance in your mind or body, such mindful breathing will help you regain your equilibrium.

I have used this calming exercise when driving, in the company of other people (without them noticing), at the movies, in meetings, and in many other situations.

Often, I have processed the disturbance in more depth later, usually when I'm alone in a safe place, reflecting on the key events of my day. Doing this gives me an opportunity to discover if there is anything deeper to my reaction. I am always keen to recognize and acknowledge any issue or emotion from the past that is still active within my psyche. To do this, I ask my guides for help. Focusing on the disturbed feeling, I ask myself, "When have I felt this before?" I notice what comes to mind—a memory, perhaps, or images, words, or sensations.

Even though these don't always make any logical sense, I continue exploring. I ask myself why these memories or images are important and how they relate to my current disturbance.

Asking questions is useful. It helps me make connections so I can understand why I reacted the way I did. Sometimes the relationship between my reaction and the past comes easily. Other times, it can take weeks or months to get the answers and make the connections. Once, I took over twenty years to gain the answer. In that case, I hadn't been ready to emotionally deal with the answer or to make the changes in my life that this new knowledge would demand.

Trust what you get and what you don't get. Your guides know what you need.

## Connecting to Your Inner Guidance and Spiritual Guides

For many, connecting to inner guidance or spiritual guides, which I am calling Source, is fairly straightforward. It really is no different to the intuitive thoughts, ideas, or messages that pop into your awareness from time to time, whether you have asked for them or not.

We can struggle to receive guidance when this connection is blocked. Source never blocks us; rather, we cut ourselves off from Source. There can be many reasons why. Skepticism about the existence of Source is one possible block. We may feel angry, either from a specific slight or loss or generally at the many hardships we have faced. We may doubt our ability to connect with Source or believe ourselves unworthy of any help or assistance from a higher power. We may fear being punished (possibly related to childhood experiences or religious indoctrination), we may fear our own vulnerability, we may be weighed down with guilt and anger, or we may simply not yet be ready to hear the truth.

If you struggle to connect, your first step is identifying any blocks and finding a way to remove them, possibly with professional help. Realize that your connection to Source is present and available even when you are not aware of it.

To connect:

- Find a quiet, safe, comfortable space where you will not be disturbed.

- Ask that only those wise beings who are focused on your higher good and the higher good of all be present.

- Relax your body by focusing on your breath, feeling a sense of expansion in your body as you breathe in. As you breathe out, focus on releasing and letting go of the air and any tension in your body. Do this by taking slow, deep breaths until you feel calm and peaceful.

- Remind yourself that Source energy is present and near and wants to connect.

- Imagine opening your heart, your arms, your whole self, to let this energy in. This is an expansive feeling. In your mind, you might see something or someone, a light perhaps. Alternatively, you might not see anything at all. You might feel something: a change, a warmth, a quickening, or an energy of some sort. Trust that feeling even if it is subtle. You might hear something: a voice, a message, music, some sound. Again, trust!

- Whether you receive any of the above indications or not, you can assume a wise energy or entity is present and ask a question. The very first thought or idea, image or impression, or feeling or sensation that emerges in your mind or body is an answer or message for you at this point in time. Take note! Usually, the answer makes immediate sense. Quite likely you have thought of it before. If the message is confusing in any way, you might need to decipher it later.

## A Few Tips

- The more often you do this exercise, the easier connecting will become. Even if nothing happens, it is worth continuing to ask for connection. Some of us have neglected this channel of communication for so long that it takes time, patience, and trust to reopen it.

- Your focus needs to be positive and trusting. Remember, we receive what we are putting out. If you don't feel open and trusting, it is a good idea to clear up any doubts you have beforehand.

- You need to be open to using your imagination, as that is the way these communications come. You are receiving nonphysical communication. Thus, it is an intuitive process.

- Most important is realizing guidance is just that: guidance. You, and only you, are responsible for the actions you take in life, whether your actions were guided or not. Don't do anything unless you are willing to take responsibility for the outcome of your actions.

## Accepting the Sovereignty of All Souls

Loving and caring people naturally feel for others and want to alleviate their suffering. But this is not always possible or advised. It is not our job to take the karmic load from another by stepping in to save them from the consequences of their actions. Each soul is on a path of learning. We need to be very clear on our motivations before we interfere in another's path.

If we want to prevent or alleviate the suffering of others because it seriously disturbs us, our motivations may be distorted. We need to ask ourselves if we are trying to avoid our own suffering. Sometimes when we witness the suffering of others, we feel upset. But this is often because some past issue of our own has been triggered and remains unresolved.

I always look closely at my own motivations to make sure my desire to help is not ego driven. I want to make sure my motivations are clean and I am following wise guidance by helping. Our wise inner guidance can be our most important ally when working out the approach that is for the highest good of all.

Practical help is sometimes called for, but there are also other ways to help those who are suffering. We do this by sending light and love:

- Close your eyes and take a few deep, slow breaths.
- Call in your guides, trusting they are present.
- Ask them to surround the sufferer or situation with loving light.
- Imagine you see the person or situation being surrounded with this nurturing, powerful light, like a ball of light energy or a column of light coming down from above, surrounding the individual, place, or situation.
- Trust that this loving light energy is alleviating any pain and turmoil by warming and comforting this person, people, or situation, giving them space to see and think clearly.

The guides have told us many times that this process, which is similar to prayer, makes a difference to suffering individuals and also to the energy of our planet.

# Stepping into Joy

Here is a way of drawing on your positive past to create a practice of feeling joy whenever you choose. As you practice this process, you will find it becomes easier and easier until you no longer need to do each step. Your objective is to be able to deliberately access joyful feelings quickly in many situations.

To learn this technique:

- Begin by finding a comfortable space where you will not be disturbed.

- Close your eyes and take a few slow, deep breaths.

- When you feel comfortable and relaxed, take a moment to recall one of the most powerful, joyful occasions in your life. You can ask your guides to help you do this.

- Immerse yourself in this joyful experience, remembering details of the occasion. Then it may only take a moment to receive the impact of these happy feelings. Breathe them in. Allow them to flow right through your body and into your heart.

- Focus on your heart. Deliberately see it expand so you feel love, joy, and gratitude for all the blessings in your life, including the rich experiences you have had and are having.

- Know that you are fulfilling your purpose, no matter what is happening on your journey. Whether you feel despair or happiness, in truth, you cannot fail to fulfill

your purpose. Although you may have believed otherwise, all experience is valuable. All is well.

- As you more easily access these joyful feelings, remember your sense of joy in other situations. You may decide
to keep expanding this ability to all sorts of circumstances, even those that are challenging.

Note: You could record these exercises in your own voice to use.
Also check the recommended resources section at the end of the
book.

# SECTION 1:
# BEFORE THE FALL

# CHAPTER 1
# BEGINNING
# THE JOURNEY

Imagine waking up in a strange bed. You can't remember what happened the night before. Your arm is numb, too heavy to lift. Gradually, you become aware of the people around you. You sense that they're trying to help, but when you open your mouth to speak, your tongue feels thick, and you can't find the words you need. Your vision blurs, and you begin to lapse in and out of consciousness. Perhaps it would be easier to just fall back to sleep.

Amnesia is terrifying. It doesn't matter why you're in the hospital—a medical incident or physical trauma. Gradually, you'll begin to knit the pieces of your life back together. But there may be some memories that are lost forever.

You've experienced this before. Do you remember when you first became aware of yourself as a small child? Our earliest memories are often elusive. Perhaps you felt confused, wondering if you really belonged here. Perhaps you asked your caretakers, "Who am I?" or "Where did I come from?" Over time, their answers sank in. They gave you a name; they told you where you were born. But wisps of suspicion remained. They couldn't answer all your questions. What were they avoiding? Where did you *really* come from? And is there something you have lost forever?

As an infant, you may not have realized that you are a soul incarnating in a human body. You might still doubt this. But in all probability, you have been on earth in a physical body before.

Even though some souls feel excited and curious when coming back to earth, others can find it unsettling. For a baby, unable to fend for itself, the world can be utterly bewildering. There are peculiar beings who make weird noises and unfamiliar places filled with strange comings and goings. Newly incarnated souls have largely forgotten who they are and don't know what they might encounter this time around.

If this is challenging for souls returning after many lifetimes on earth, imagine the experience of those souls who have never incarnated here before. They find themselves encased in physical bodies that limit their movement. They are surrounded by a cacophony of intrusive sounds. Strange entities flit in and out of their vision, and every contact seems charged with intense emotions. Everything is new and potentially threatening. One can assume they find their early incarnations both confusing and confronting.

Although you have taken this journey yourself, you have probably forgotten what it was like.

Before we begin exploring the soul's journey through many lifetimes, we need answers to some pertinent questions. What is a soul? What do we mean by nonphysical? Who were we before we came to earth? Where did we come from? Why did we decide to come here? Were we prepared for this journey, and how did we begin? What was it like when we arrived here, and how did we cope?

Feeling breathless? Good—let's plunge right in!

## Nature of Souls

What is a soul? Pretty much whatever you want it to be—and there's the problem. Many people imagine souls to be light and free-spirited. Above all, they believe souls to be essentially virtuous. But as I have discovered, souls can become lost over the course of many lifetimes. They may return to earth time and time again, creating havoc and wreaking destruction.

If you want to understand what it really means to be a soul, look around at the people you know. Each one is a soul inhabiting a human body. And all the varied qualities you see in others—whether wholesome, devilish, or indifferent—reflect the state of their souls.

Before their first incarnation, souls are neither good nor bad. They are simply possibilities—aspects of Source that have chosen to experience life on our planet. Because souls are nonphysical, incarnation presents a challenge. They need to step down in vibration until they resonate with the earth system. Before they meld with a human body, they have already begun to change. They have opened themselves up to living in a system with many choices—all with consequences.

We refer to souls as nonphysical because we cannot perceive them with our physical senses. Humans have limitations that souls do not. When a soul incarnates as a human, it takes on these limitations. For example, the human eye can only see 0.0035 percent of the electromagnetic spectrum. We know our hearing range is limited—dogs and bats can hear frequencies we cannot. There are chemicals and gases that we cannot taste and smell. Our feelings and emotions are like an unexplored continent that we don't know how to navigate.

It is possible that souls and the nonphysical world exist at a subtle level of physicality that is too ethereal for us to detect. Data collected over years of research suggests that the universe is largely composed of dark energy (68 percent) and dark matter (27 percent).[3] Physics tells us that without dark matter the universe would fly apart, while dark energy drives its accelerating expansion. The visible cosmos only accounts for 5 percent of the

3. "Dark Energy, Dark Matter," What We Study, NASA, accessed April 29, 2021, https://science.nasa.gov/astrophysics/focus-areas/what-is-dark -energy.

universe. But scientists cannot see, touch, or identify either dark matter or dark energy. So far, no instruments have been able to detect them.

## Accessing the Nonphysical Universe

When people enter a hypnotic trance during regressions, they can access elements of this invisible cosmos. They visit the afterlife and other realms. They interact with friends, relatives, and celestial beings. Being in trance allows them to bypass the five senses and access their sixth sense, or third eye. I call it an intuitive sense.

The invisible cosmos includes a dimension close to the earth, which is the place the soul calls home. Michael Newton called it our "life between lives."[4] This is a little misleading because Newton eventually discovered that the soul remains in this dimension even while incarnated. Let's pause for a moment and take that in. What actually inhabits and animates our physical body is only an investment of energy from our larger soul. While we are living here on earth, another aspect of our greater self remains in another dimension.

This means there is a powerful relationship between the nonphysical realm and the physical earth. In combination, these form the earth system. A soul incarnating on earth has come from the nonphysical realms of the earth system, also known as the afterlife, the soul's home, or our life between lives.

## Duality

To our senses, the physical world seems dense and solid. While it is often beautiful, it is also potentially dangerous. To survive,

---

4. Michael Newton, *Journey of Souls: Case Studies of Life Between Lives* (St. Paul, MN: Llewellyn Publications, 2004) 3.

we must remain aware of the world around us. Because we rely so much on others, we need to know if they will help us or harm us. Are they sick or healthy, happy or miserable, kind or mean? Because our bodies are vulnerable, we need to check the weather before we step outside. Will it be hot or cold, calm or windy, wet or sunny? When we cross the street, we know to watch for cars—are they moving or stationary? If they're moving, are they travelling fast or slow, forward or backward? There is so much to notice, and it demands our full attention.

We come to realize that our world is full of opposites. Up and down, hard and soft. The most important distinction we draw is between ourselves and everything else, between *I* and *not I*. We experience reality as a set of relationships between ourselves and the rest of the world, and as another highly complex set of relationships between all the different elements we perceive in the external world: people, nature, events, and things. Each element exists relative to every other element. This is where the concept of contrast or duality comes in. It implies our separation as individuals as well as our interdependence with the rest of the world.

The whole is the combination of all these contrasts—me and you, dark and light, hot and cold. But our consciousness cannot easily hold everything together. The image below demonstrates how we can only focus on one thing at a time. You can see the two faces, or you can see the vase. As much as you try to see them both together, all you can do is quickly flick your focus from one impression to the other.

Of course, we need to perceive all the elements of this image before we can visualize the vase or the two faces. We are whole even though our consciousness is playing a game of separation. For a few moments, some clients transcend this game.

Jane found herself in a state of oneness after reliving a challenging past life.

*There is just so much love. If we could just live in that love. They [spirit beings] are always around. I am feeling the love and it is not just them. There is a greater love, and they are part of that. It is like a big space of nothing and everything. After that initial overwhelming high of love, this feels like space, evenness, nothingness, empty and full at the same time, like good and bad, whole and separate.*

I ask if that means there is no duality.

*Yes. That's right. It is everything—all that is. You cannot stay here forever. There is nothing attached to it—no space, no pattern, no emotion. And yet I sense a lot of humor in this space and in the duality. The whole concept is funny, almost like it is a cosmic joke.*

The whole, as well as our sense of separation, are opposites. Perhaps that is the joke. We are whole, but to play and to experience life, we need to be separate. There are two lessons to be drawn from Jane's experience. First, she retains her identity while being immersed in those feelings of love. She is whole and separate at the same time. However, because Jane was immersed in that sense of connection, she was not fully aware of her individual identity. It's just lingering in the background. Secondly, this experience came after she had relived a traumatic past life. Perhaps her ecstatic sense of wholeness was the culmination of all the challenges she had endured.

Other clients who have glimpsed the celestial struggled to describe the experience. They used words such as oneness, expansion, peace, connection, completeness, and timelessness. Boundaries disappeared and, for a moment, the "I" disappeared. I had thought this was probably as close as we could get to understanding wholeness until one client, Amber, had an unusual experience.

In her regression, Amber became an eagle, flying over a valley of volcanos and lava that had destroyed her nest and fledglings. Pierced by a deep sense of loss, she felt that her life lacked all purpose—until she saw the valley open to the sea and she came into a bright white light.

*I feel my third eye is opening up. I have been guided to the white light, and I feel peace. I am able to see the sum of all parts and more than the dualistic nature of things.*

*I am seeing through the two eyes of the bird on each side of my head, which is both sides of everything and the sum of all parts as well. Each eye moves independently on each side of my head, and I see the whole with my third eye. The bright light is a place where it can all exist together rather than feeling torn about the details. That is really expansive. At the base of everything, there is no separation, and that is an expanded feeling. It is very reassuring.*

Amber later described this experience as life changing. While Jane felt consumed by love, Amber remained aware of the movement of the eagle's individual eyes as well as its intuitive ability to see all. She was simultaneously aware of her duality and the wholeness.

This is the paradox of spirituality. If our consciousness were to be fully absorbed in the oneness, we would lose any concept of our separate identity. But as soon as we develop a concept of self, we experience everything else as separate. By definition, any awareness of our personal existence seems to require the experience, or perhaps the illusion, of separation from the whole.

We may imagine souls as being spiritual and ethereal in composition. Nevertheless, they, like humans, are playing this separation game too, as one client explained.

*A soul is a point of consciousness, a point of understanding, independent, with a separate consciousness. It has its own thoughts, is able to communicate with others, and does.*

One of my clients, Jasmine, was worried about returning to her life between lives. Who would she be, she wondered, once she entered the nonphysical realm?

*Recently, I feared that being on the other side was all lovely and light. They are reassuring me that my wicked sense of humor has a place, and personality and individuality still exist there. There is dark and there is light, and both are accepted.*

Another client, Ethan, wanted to know what it was like being in spirit and if there were contrasts as there are on earth. He was told that, "When we are all one, there is no fun." Ethan understood this to mean that separation exists in the life between lives and beyond. Without contrast, existence is boring. Souls make decisions without knowing how their choice will turn out. Risk does not disappear when we return to our life between lives after death. Contrast and some level of risk remain, even after we re-emerge with our higher self.

## Why Incarnate on Planet Earth?

Our universe offers an experience of separation that makes life interesting. But there is something different about incarnating on earth. The experience of separation and contrast is so extreme, we forget who we are. Earth has a heavier vibration than other places.[5] Indeed, most humans remain unaware of the nonphysical dimensions. In any case, while in trance, many of my clients marvel at the unusual nature of our planet—its solidity and the deeper contrasts that exist here as opposed to other places or dimensions.

All my clients are experienced souls. They may have come to earth as young souls thousands of years ago, experiencing many incarnations since they first arrived. Others came here after incarnating on other planets or in other dimensions. For both groups, their early incarnations on earth can come as a shock. While souls choose to come to earth, none of them know what they'll discover until they actually live here.

Rosaria elucidates her larger soul's reasons for coming to earth to incarnate.

> There is something very distracting about the solidity of the earth environment. It makes it harder to remember the game. The energy is so dense and solid. I knew about the amnesia, but I didn't really understand. It was a nonphysical knowing, and that is not the same. Earth has been a bit of a shock.

Another client, Penny, explains how she and two close soulmates came into the earth system to incarnate.

> We have stepped down in frequency to be souls in the earth plane, and then we have stepped down in frequency again to be physical.

---

5. Newton, *Destiny of Souls*, 104–105.

Penny and her soulmates have accepted having limitations at the soul level, and then have accepted even greater limitations as humans.

Valencia had experience in other places. She describes her attraction to earth.

*Earth has a level of energy that you don't get on other planets. You can go into levels that are deeper and darker. There is something special about this planet because of its level of lower frequency and the freedom of choice. It is a huge step down for us who come from places that are less physical. I came in spite of that because I felt the need to experience the heavier levels.*

The "I" Valencia refers to is her larger self, which gained a wealth of experience in other dimensions before first incarnating on earth. Many clients during their regressions seem to attain a higher perspective and speak as their larger, more knowledgeable self.

Akali asks her guides why she feels she doesn't belong on earth.

*My guide is laughing. "You wanted to evolve quickly, didn't you? Planet earth is the toughest school, the best university. The curriculum is tough."*

Akali wonders where she came from.

*I am getting that I am a very old soul. I haven't been on this planet a lot. I have evolved on other planets in other universes that are beyond our human imagination. I have only had five incarnations on this planet. I chose the best university for continuing my learning.*

Many eternal beings, like Akali's greater self, choose to incarnate here because it is a challenging and rewarding school. In many regressions, the guides emphasize that humans do not need to justify their presence on the planet. Just choosing to incarnate here is a courageous decision no matter how you live your life.

# Beginning Souls

In Michael Newton's book *Destiny of Souls: New Case Studies of Life Between Lives*, his clients describe newly created souls as "hatchlings."[6] One of my clients, Sophia, refers to them as "baby souls."

*Baby souls, when born, are just as cute as human babies. Everyone gets fussy about little adorable baby souls, just like they do with human babies on earth. A new little soul is a lovely, cute, playful being, like a baby kitten—so sweet and vulnerable.*

*Like babies on earth, new souls are nurtured and protected as they adjust to the energies and begin their schooling. The soul needs to learn first before incarnating as a human baby.*

*We can't go to earth at that stage; we are too small. I can feel myself as that little energy. We have a lot to learn first. We have to grow up, like being in school. We are too vulnerable to be put in a body. We are in a fog, and we need the fog to protect us while we learn to get stronger and grow into a more capable soul.*

The little soul's foggy confusion is protective. No one can know everything at once. Each soul is exposed to new experiences, information, and semi-physical places before incarnating on earth. This includes simulated practice, which is not the same as actual incarnation.

Another client, Easha, learns that her soul is a teacher of young souls. In the place her soul calls home, she sits on an orb surrounded by circles of many young souls. Some of the classes are for souls who have yet to incarnate, and some are for those in between their early incarnations.

*All are meditating and absorbing the light. They are eager to learn. I am their teacher and mentor, and they depend on me and trust me. I feel the energy from the orb travelling outward in a frequency that*

---

6. Newton, *Destiny of Souls*, 128–130.

*makes us one. We go through sensations and observe them and let them go. It is like waves on a beach coming and going. It is so familiar.*

*We practice this and eventually the group progresses to something else, and I have another new group of souls. Some returning from earth have dimmed light and are happy to be back home. They are learning to be calm and balance their emotions. With the energy of the orb and practice, they are recharged and brighter.*

Easha notes that there are other souls who are more of a challenge to work with.

*They are not stable; they change very quickly, like being indecisive. It is in their nature. They have a lot of energy. They like to experiment. They are willful and changeable. They trust me because I don't tell them what to do.*

From Easha's description, we learn that new souls have different characters and qualities that can affect their behavior.

As pointed out earlier, new souls seem to be very delicate. They need to become accustomed to being in a physical body. During her regressions, Rachel recalls her first incarnations.

*In the beginning, I had three lives to become familiar with being physical. I had to get used to having a heartbeat and a solid form and moving in a body with gravity and weight. I see a strange landscape of curved rocks. I was some sort of unusual animal. In the same place, I am now an alien in a humanoid form but not a Homo sapiens. Now, I have a smaller body, a being like a bird, but I feel a heaviness in the heart. Flying is hard. I am not used to the wings. When I am older and bigger, it is not so hard, but gravity is still challenging. My guides are asking me if I want to do this because I am going to be put into a Homo sapiens life. I say yes. It is experience. I feel determined and resolved.*

*pt fitting in as a given. I am getting that these people are part
...tended soul group, and we have been incarnating together for a
...e. I feel connected again. I can physically feel the connection of
...t chakra to Source, and now it is expanding. Particles of gold
...ing over me, gently, like a mist. A path is opening up in front
...d I am floating along it. I feel I am suspended, and I received
...ge: "Welcome."*

*...guides are saying that this is a significant life because it is
...ne the importance of being connected to others but also recog-
...that fear is not a state of integrity. I didn't need to feel any fear
...I was comfortable being a part of the group. I wasn't resistant
...thers were. If they left, they lost the safety of belonging. It is
...nt to know when you are surrendering and that surrendering is
...l feeling.*

...night note that both Cody and Kathleen had little fear in
...ly lives. They didn't feel like they were submitting because
...e to the rules of the group was so inherent and natural.
...onnected to their community and its members, they felt
...protected.

...p affinity is also evident in the members' relationships with
...ers and departed ancestors. In this life, Kathleen has com-
...pect for the leader, who is responsible for the group's wel-
...d Cody, too, is respectful, expressing how he feels about
...ho die—not just his ancestors, but the lonely ones who had

*...e honor those who die. Our dead are always with us. We are con-
...l to our ancestors, and we honor them directly. The ones who walk
...we honor in spirit. We are connected by our stories. They provide
...ith perspective of their journeys as we learn through our dreams.*

The adjustment needed to begin incarnating on earth is a big step, even for those souls who have had previous experiences on other planets or in other dimensions.

## Entry into Earth Life

As humans, we first incarnate on planet earth as innocent beings, dropped into unfamiliar territory without a map or a manual. Before we were born, we agreed to one specific condition: that once incarnated, we must forget our larger soul-self. Our soul wanted to experience human form so strongly that it accepted this restriction. This is why we can sometimes lack purpose in our lives—because we have forgotten the depths of our soul's desire.

We arrive open and curious. Even though we retain some sense of our divine nature, we are here on the planet to integrate with our dense physical body. As a newborn, we don't even know we have a physical body, and many months pass before we realize that our body is separate from everything and everyone else. Gradually, we become aware of our physical nature, developing our ability to use our bodies.

Physical bodies need food, water, and shelter. We must learn how to provide these essentials for ourselves. Also, the physical world is dangerous. We are naïve, and many difficult lessons await us.

It is not surprising that in early lives many souls choose to be born into tight-knit communities with established customs, prescribed laws, and strict standards of behavior. The group teaches us how to survive in a threatening environment. It also fosters close connection to others and gives protection to members. Usually, these groups have a strong spiritual connection expressed through religion, sacred songs and dances, and a close connection to the natural world. This resonates with souls new to the earth because group rituals and worship connect them back to Source energy. Because they thrive on connection to others, nature, and spirit, the lack of individual freedom does not worry them. Three cases illustrate the attraction to life in these protective communities.

During his regression, Cody is taken back to an early life as an Indigenous Australian.

*I am male, a provider who hunts and gathers. Food is monotonous but abundant. We don't have a lot of ups and downs in life. We live connected to the land. We have traditions but not rules. We don't need rules. The traditions are the way we do things, the way we celebrate and honor our ancestors.*

I ask what happens if someone doesn't follow the traditions.

*We might have to cast them out for the sake of the rest of us. We don't survive as much as we exist. We don't have the fear of survival. We have our challenges—lightning, storms, and fire—but we have our songs, our medicines, and our families.*

*Disruption does not serve the group. There is an understanding that any disrupters are not welcome, and they leave. We call them the lonely ones. It is not an active casting out. It is a natural process. We exclude them, and they choose to leave. They are still family, and we celebrate their choice. We honor them in our songs, in the earth, and in the stars. We grieve and we let go.*

*Some members will manage better than others, but it is a lesson in acceptance—accepting the grief, the choice, and the loss. The lonely ones leave because their energy doesn't fit with the community. They are with us in word but not in spirit. We know that if they stay, in the long-term, their actions will not serve us. We are one, tuned in together, and harmonious.*

*During our early incarnations living in a tight-knit community, we accept our mutual reliance on others. Our interdependence also extends*

*to our thinking. Generally, we co[...] group and quite naturally adopt its [...]*

In our second case, Kathleen sh[...] ral interdependence is for her in an [...] pily in a large, close-knit communi[...] groups.

*I see a bright blue sky and the su[...] ing down on barren, old mountains [...] is dry and sandy, like a desert, but th[...]*

*I am a young female of twelve at[...] seeing a few skin shelters of nomadic [...] twenty or thirty goats, and it is an im[...] nify wealth and give milk.*

We go to another scene.

*I am inside and there is a gatherin[...] have ever seen before, probably about [...] I am about fifteen, sitting in amongst t[...] fire pits, and we are eating food that has [...]*

*We are here to pay allegiance to our [...] he looks after us. He is the head, and [...] underneath him. This gathering doesn't [...] every several years. The timing is based [...] We then go off on the nomadic routes th[...] somewhere in the Middle East.*

*I am getting an understanding of the [...] If you are not part of it, you cannot sur[...] hand-to-mouth struggle. I have been lectu[...] is deeply instilled, especially the emphasis [...] in. The gathering is to reinforce the rules [...] as sharing information.*

Interdependence is essential for survival when you have little experience of being physical and facing harsh conditions on earth.

Religious conclaves also provide a safe place for the newly incarnated soul. These communities are well-established, tightly structured, and allow members to engage in spiritual practices. In our third case, Joyce retains a strong connection to God in her life as a monk named Brother Martin.

*I am in a monk's outfit with peaked shoes, like slippers. I am around forty, with a tonsure hairstyle. I am standing here looking at this room, which is like a cellar with solid arches of red brick. I feel lightness. Something important happened here. I am calm and smiling, sensing something majestic but not knowing what it could be. I am picking up energy that is happy and joyful; actually, it is a calm joy.*

*I am curious, wondering why I feel so much peace in this place. It is a sacred place. I had a glimpse of someone dying here. [Cries.] I have a sense of quiet joy.*

*Even though no outside light comes into this room, there is a lightness here.*

*Now I see the past when I was here with a dying man. The man is my master, dressed in white, a beautiful being who has been a guiding light for me. He is a teacher in the monastery and has been a loving presence. I am there remembering the beauty of my master's passing with much love. Not sad but happy.*

*As a monk, I have been with many people as they died. I remember one man with his grieving wife beside him. I am holding his hand, expressing love, nothing more, just love. I feel happy for his passing. It is his time. I keep getting a sense of the beauty of leaving. I know, without a shadow of a doubt, that the afterlife is a beautiful place and dying is a beautiful experience.*

In a scene later in this life, Brother Martin is dying in the same room where his master passed.

*I am lying in the red brick vault and my protégé is there. He is thin with a long nose. He feels a lot of love and respect toward me, and I am feeling love for him. He is ready but unsure. He feels my energy and joy, much the same as I did when I was in his position. He is feeling the human sadness of us parting but the beauty of me leaving.*

*I am anointing him. An anointing is just putting the hands on the anointed one's shoulders. We know a transference is taking place. The energy is passed with the thought: "This is your path now."*

After passing, Joyce as her soul-self realizes why Brother Martin was so peaceful, loving, and accepting.

*In that life as Brother Martin, I wondered why people [on earth] were angry and unhappy. I could be loving with these people because I saw dying as beautiful. I wasn't afraid like others were. I didn't have complete amnesia. I was deeply connected to God and didn't feel violent or passionate. I was feeling too much love.*

Because Brother Martin had not completely forgotten his soul origins, he retained a strong connection to Source energy. His attention was still largely focused on heaven, his soul's home. This is not surprising, for he was a young soul and a devoted monk. However, his ethereal presence meant that he could not relate to human emotions such as fear, grief, and anger. This limited his ability to help those who were lost in grief. After this life, Brother Martin's soul decided to experience these emotions in depth so he could relate more closely with others. For many centuries, he planned and experienced some extremely challenging lives.

## Masculine and Feminine Energies

Another focus of souls in their early lives is expressing feminine and masculine qualities in a pure form. Often, we choose to take

The adjustment needed to begin incarnating on earth is a big step, even for those souls who have had previous experiences on other planets or in other dimensions.

## Entry into Earth Life

As humans, we first incarnate on planet earth as innocent beings, dropped into unfamiliar territory without a map or a manual. Before we were born, we agreed to one specific condition: that once incarnated, we must forget our larger soul-self. Our soul wanted to experience human form so strongly that it accepted this restriction. This is why we can sometimes lack purpose in our lives—because we have forgotten the depths of our soul's desire.

We arrive open and curious. Even though we retain some sense of our divine nature, we are here on the planet to integrate with our dense physical body. As a newborn, we don't even know we have a physical body, and many months pass before we realize that our body is separate from everything and everyone else. Gradually, we become aware of our physical nature, developing our ability to use our bodies.

Physical bodies need food, water, and shelter. We must learn how to provide these essentials for ourselves. Also, the physical world is dangerous. We are naïve, and many difficult lessons await us.

It is not surprising that in early lives many souls choose to be born into tight-knit communities with established customs, prescribed laws, and strict standards of behavior. The group teaches us how to survive in a threatening environment. It also fosters close connection to others and gives protection to members. Usually, these groups have a strong spiritual connection expressed through religion, sacred songs and dances, and a close connection to the natural world. This resonates with souls new to the earth because group rituals and worship connect them back to Source energy. Because they thrive on connection to others, nature, and spirit, the lack of individual freedom does not worry them. Three cases illustrate the attraction to life in these protective communities.

During his regression, Cody is taken back to an early life as an Indigenous Australian.

*I am male, a provider who hunts and gathers. Food is monotonous but abundant. We don't have a lot of ups and downs in life. We live connected to the land. We have traditions but not rules. We don't need rules. The traditions are the way we do things, the way we celebrate and honor our ancestors.*

I ask what happens if someone doesn't follow the traditions.

*We might have to cast them out for the sake of the rest of us. We don't survive as much as we exist. We don't have the fear of survival. We have our challenges—lightning, storms, and fire—but we have our songs, our medicines, and our families.*

*Disruption does not serve the group. There is an understanding that any disrupters are not welcome, and they leave. We call them the lonely ones. It is not an active casting out. It is a natural process. We exclude them, and they choose to leave. They are still family, and we celebrate their choice. We honor them in our songs, in the earth, and in the stars. We grieve and we let go.*

*Some members will manage better than others, but it is a lesson in acceptance—accepting the grief, the choice, and the loss. The lonely ones leave because their energy doesn't fit with the community. They are with us in word but not in spirit. We know that if they stay, in the long-term, their actions will not serve us. We are one, tuned in together, and harmonious.*

*During our early incarnations living in a tight-knit community, we accept our mutual reliance on others. Our interdependence also extends* to our thinking. Generally, we concur with the collective mind of the group and quite naturally adopt its rules and practices.

In our second case, Kathleen shows how comfortable and natural interdependence is for her in an early incarnation. She lives happily in a large, close-knit community made up of smaller nomadic groups.

*I see a bright blue sky and the sun, in the middle of the day, shining down on barren, old mountains worn down over time. The ground is dry and sandy, like a desert, but there are patches of thin grass.*

*I am a young female of twelve attending to a rabble of goats. I am seeing a few skin shelters of nomadic families. I am happy tending the twenty or thirty goats, and it is an important job because the goats signify wealth and give milk.*

We go to another scene.

*I am inside and there is a gathering of many people, more than I have ever seen before, probably about fifty in a communal tent. Now I am about fifteen, sitting in amongst the crowd at the back. There are fire pits, and we are eating food that has been cooked in them.*

*We are here to pay allegiance to our leader. We admire him because he looks after us. He is the head, and each group has a leader who is underneath him. This gathering doesn't happen very often, only once every several years. The timing is based on the stars and the seasons. We then go off on the nomadic routes that each group follows. We are somewhere in the Middle East.*

*I am getting an understanding of the importance of group cohesion. If you are not part of it, you cannot survive because life is already a hand-to-mouth struggle. I have been lectured about the rules, and this is deeply instilled, especially the emphasis on expulsion if you don't fit in. The gathering is to reinforce the rules for the survival of all as well as sharing information.*

*I accept fitting in as a given. I am getting that these people are part of my extended soul group, and we have been incarnating together for a long time. I feel connected again. I can physically feel the connection of my heart chakra to Source, and now it is expanding. Particles of gold are washing over me, gently, like a mist. A path is opening up in front of me and I am floating along it. I feel I am suspended, and I received a message: "Welcome."*

*The guides are saying that this is a significant life because it is telling me the importance of being connected to others but also recognizing that fear is not a state of integrity. I didn't need to feel any fear because I was comfortable being a part of the group. I wasn't resistant while others were. If they left, they lost the safety of belonging. It is important to know when you are surrendering and that surrendering is a joyful feeling.*

You might note that both Cody and Kathleen had little fear in these early lives. They didn't feel like they were submitting because adherence to the rules of the group was so inherent and natural. Being connected to their community and its members, they felt safe and protected.

Group affinity is also evident in the members' relationships with their elders and departed ancestors. In this life, Kathleen has complete respect for the leader, who is responsible for the group's welfare. And Cody, too, is respectful, expressing how he feels about those who die—not just his ancestors, but the lonely ones who had to leave.

*We honor those who die. Our dead are always with us. We are connected to our ancestors, and we honor them directly. The ones who walk away we honor in spirit. We are connected by our stories. They provide us with perspective of their journeys as we learn through our dreams.*

Interdependence is essential for survival when you have little experience of being physical and facing harsh conditions on earth.

Religious conclaves also provide a safe place for the newly incarnated soul. These communities are well-established, tightly structured, and allow members to engage in spiritual practices. In our third case, Joyce retains a strong connection to God in her life as a monk named Brother Martin.

*I am in a monk's outfit with peaked shoes, like slippers. I am around forty, with a tonsure hairstyle. I am standing here looking at this room, which is like a cellar with solid arches of red brick. I feel lightness. Something important happened here. I am calm and smiling, sensing something majestic but not knowing what it could be. I am picking up energy that is happy and joyful; actually, it is a calm joy.*

*I am curious, wondering why I feel so much peace in this place. It is a sacred place. I had a glimpse of someone dying here. [Cries.] I have a sense of quiet joy.*

*Even though no outside light comes into this room, there is a lightness here.*

*Now I see the past when I was here with a dying man. The man is my master, dressed in white, a beautiful being who has been a guiding light for me. He is a teacher in the monastery and has been a loving presence. I am there remembering the beauty of my master's passing with much love. Not sad but happy.*

*As a monk, I have been with many people as they died. I remember one man with his grieving wife beside him. I am holding his hand, expressing love, nothing more, just love. I feel happy for his passing. It is his time. I keep getting a sense of the beauty of leaving. I know, without a shadow of a doubt, that the afterlife is a beautiful place and dying is a beautiful experience.*

In a scene later in this life, Brother Martin is dying in the same room where his master passed.

*I am lying in the red brick vault and my protégé is there. He is thin with a long nose. He feels a lot of love and respect toward me, and I am feeling love for him. He is ready but unsure. He feels my energy and joy, much the same as I did when I was in his position. He is feeling the human sadness of us parting but the beauty of me leaving.*

*I am anointing him. An anointing is just putting the hands on the anointed one's shoulders. We know a transference is taking place. The energy is passed with the thought: "This is your path now."*

After passing, Joyce as her soul-self realizes why Brother Martin was so peaceful, loving, and accepting.

*In that life as Brother Martin, I wondered why people [on earth] were angry and unhappy. I could be loving with these people because I saw dying as beautiful. I wasn't afraid like others were. I didn't have complete amnesia. I was deeply connected to God and didn't feel violent or passionate. I was feeling too much love.*

Because Brother Martin had not completely forgotten his soul origins, he retained a strong connection to Source energy. His attention was still largely focused on heaven, his soul's home. This is not surprising, for he was a young soul and a devoted monk. However, his ethereal presence meant that he could not relate to human emotions such as fear, grief, and anger. This limited his ability to help those who were lost in grief. After this life, Brother Martin's soul decided to experience these emotions in depth so he could relate more closely with others. For many centuries, he planned and experienced some extremely challenging lives.

## Masculine and Feminine Energies

Another focus of souls in their early lives is expressing feminine and masculine qualities in a pure form. Often, we choose to take

on the same gender in a series of lifetimes in order to develop the essential elements of masculinity or femininity. As we progress through our many lives on earth, we eventually learn how to integrate and balance both male and female energies.

Terry, who you will meet in later chapters, mentions his development of protective male attributes in one of his sessions.

*I just got a glimpse of my first life on earth. It was 25,000 BCE. I see a small settlement where I lived until I was two years old, when I died of the cold. But that life was useful, just a little taste of earth. The majority of my lives after that were peaceful, rural lives. I only fought when I needed to protect my family or community.*

Fighting helped these men develop their physical skills and their sense of courage, which they needed to maximize their chance of survival. Strength and courage, used as a protective force, is important to souls wishing to engender healthy masculine energy.

Valentina experienced a life as a male in a matriarchy. In this life, the women were graceful, loving, and the source of sacred teachings. The men were strong, masculine, and protective. The men greatly respected the wisdom of the women and took their role as protectors very seriously. Valentina learned the difference between male and female energies and discovered the source of violence.

*Female energy is like a peaceful stream, while male energy is like big waves and excitement. Male energy can be explosive. But heartless killing doesn't come from male energy. It comes from emptiness.*

Melody had an early life in a community where pure feminine energy could be expressed.

*It was a very exciting life, a feminine life of Picts and Celts worshipping Mother Earth and the goddess. It was a powerful time for females. Women were priestesses and medicine women, highly respected*

41

*and a little feared. Men would ask for their wisdom. I liked that life and that form.*

In our early lives, we often focus on expressing one gender in its raw, instinctive form to develop familiarity with that particular energy. Our long-term aim is to integrate the qualities of both male and female energy so that whatever gender we express in a life, we know how to balance it with its opposite.

## Conclusion

As souls new to the earth, we arrive filled with hope and excitement. We are keen to experience this place of beauty and extreme contrast. We have been nurtured and lovingly schooled. Our preparation has included practice in simulations and on gentle planets. But the nonphysical lacks the heavy vibrations of earth. We come here as naïve souls inhabiting sensitive bodies, not knowing how to live in a place of such rich contrasts. Being too ignorant to make wise decisions, we choose life experiences that will help us adjust to the earth energies.

Close-knit, tightly regulated communities provide certainty, safety, and opportunities for young souls. We develop physical and emotional skills while surviving in a potentially hostile environment. The community fosters connection to each other and to the group. Its rituals and customs reflect a shared belief in an unseen world, populated by spirits or gods. We learn the ways of our gender and submit to the wisdom of the elders, respecting their care and guidance.

Yes, we face difficulties in our early incarnations, but they are relatively mild. As we adjust to the earth system, the challenges become greater, our lessons harder and more disorienting. In our next chapter, we see how some souls have faced these challenges.

# CHAPTER 2
# GETTING LOST

For many years, I worried about earthbound spirits. When we die, our spirit is released from our body. It contains the energy and nature of our soul, as well as a lifetime's worth of experience. Usually, our spirit passes over to our life between lives—but not always. Sometimes, we become stuck in the earth plane—usually when we're tangled up in the trauma or confusion of our death.

Early in my career, one of my clients became fearful during our session. She recounted the terror of being mortally stabbed. This occurred in a previous life when she had been incarnated as male. He refused to accept his death. Instead of ascending to his life between lives, his spirit found itself trapped in an ongoing fight for survival.

Later, many of my clients reported similar traumas, which they relived with an emotional intensity, making the death seem vividly real. Once the pain and terror were released, they felt light, peaceful, and liberated. When I investigated further, I realised they had released aspects of themselves who had become stuck at the end of their previous lives.

I wondered why so many spirits became trapped at death in some sort of suspended state that seemed like purgatory. Could there be a flaw in the makeup of the earth system? Eventually, I encountered clients whose regressions helped me make sense of this confusion.

We come to earth having forgotten the details of our previous incarnations, which is commonly called "the amnesia." But not everything is forgotten. How could we evolve if that was the case? Something must be retained. In this chapter, we explore how this works.

We become lost by cutting ourselves off from Source and others to varying degrees. In fact, we are always connected to these higher energies, just as our phone connects us to the outside world. We decide who we call, how often, and whether to take a call or not. We can ask for help or go it alone. In this analogy, regardless of our choice, the connection is still there. It is the same in the nonphysical world. Lost spirits can forget or refuse their connection to Source. Focused on survival, some are still fighting for their lives and others are lost and confused, unaware that their body has died.

The cases in this chapter are about people who have been lost. People coming to see me have been lost and are now in the process of re-establishing healthy relationships with themselves, others, and Source rather than descending further into darkness. However, their stories can show us how souls become lost and stay lost. We learn how their choices affected their subsequent lives. We also gain a glimpse of how souls emerge, although this is addressed in more detail in later chapters.

## Lost from Shock

Our personality, our beliefs, and our focus shape our experience of dying. For example, people who cling tightly to the material world will intensely resist their death. This tension can bind the spirit to the earth plane even after the body has long since turned to dust.

During past life and life between lives regressions, we relive at least one death. Our reaction to dying becomes clear to us. Some of us accept death, while others fight back. Some don't want to die, and others feel shocked and confused. When we resist death we leave a residue of energy—an earthbound spirit—which can influence the trajectory of our subsequent lives.

In her regression, Freda was taken back to a past life specifically to release an energetic remnant left over from her death in that life. Previously, she had harboured a pervasive sense of feeling lost, which had worsened over time.

In the early twentieth century past life, Freda was a teenager living in a Quaker community in the Midwest of the US. When a vicious storm came, she and her mother huddled together under a table. Freda reports what happened after a tornado suddenly struck.

*Why am I here? I can't work out where I am. I feel lost. I don't know what is going on. Where is my mother? I cannot find her. I am confused.*

Holding her mother tightly as they cowered underneath the kitchen table, Freda felt the terror rising in her chest when the house began to shake. She was so focused on riding out the storm, she did not even realize she had died. Her guides explain how this happens.

*When the death is quick, we can go into a limbo state. It gives us an opportunity to calm down. The guides are watching. They know you are confused, and they want you to calm down on your own before you are aware of anything else.*

I ask if there was a part of the young girl's energy still stuck in the illusion of the Midwest until we did the regression.

*Yes. That is why I asked, "Why am I here?" I was still stuck there. That is why we were taken to that life, to free me. It is like a memory, and now we are bringing in a new perspective.*

When our spirit is lost, we can feel lost in our current life. Some people have trouble navigating, worrying about getting lost in their hometown or city. For example, some don't know which direction is north. These clients usually tell me they have lost their way in life. I am not surprised when we discover one or more past lives where they died without knowing where to go, finding themselves stuck.

## Fear Carried Over

Some beliefs humans hold are fundamentally faulty. For example, many people believe they are nothing more than their physical body, meaning they expect to experience nothing after they die. Even those with a concept of a creator can be trapped in an illusion, fearing they will be punished or sent to hell at the end of their life. Either view can create a substantial block to moving on after death, which then impacts their subsequent lives.

Because we create our reality, if we believe there is nothing after death, that is what we shall find: nothingness. Unfortunately, this is common. I have encountered hundreds of spirits caught in this state.

Linda never married and lives alone. Through her interest in past lives, she has established contact with her spirit guide. She knows some of her past lives have been traumatic. Before we begin her regression, she shares how she feels.

*I am anxious, afraid of death. I am ruled by fear. I fear I have done something bad. There is a feeling in me that I have dabbled in the dark forces and done terrible things.*

*I suddenly died in a fire in one past life. In WWII, I was in the Resistance in France, and I was shot. I was the chief of an American Indigenous clan in another [life] when I was overpowered and killed by my current brother. I decided I would never want to be subjected to that again. That decision has affected me ever since. I am judgmental and shut down. My guide told me, "That decision has closed your heart." I don't want to stay closed.*

Making such an emphatic decision—"I shall never be over-powered by anyone again"—can imprint our soul and close our hearts. Once the soul is imprinted, the impact of that decision can carry over into subsequent lives. Being constantly vigilant for any hint of aggression creates a mindset of distrust—the opposite of an open heart. When we draw our boundaries so tight, we end up feeling anxious in many situations. While we may fend off aggressive people, we can also feel threatened by those who are simply self-confident, assertive, or decisive, not to mention those who hold views that contradict our beliefs. The intensity of our reaction toward others reflects the severity of our original trauma.

Linda has been affected in her current life by this decision to never be overpowered. Now she is taken to a past life where that decision also played out. In this life, Linda's soul is a miner called Rob.

To transition clients into a past life, I often suggest they move through a beautiful tunnel. When I suggest this to Linda at the beginning of her regression, she immediately feels afraid. I have inadvertently triggered her fear of being overwhelmed.

*It's like a railway tunnel. It is big enough for me to go through, but I feel like I am confined and trapped. Now it is too small to fit through, too enclosed to move. I don't want to be in a narrow space where it feels like all is tumbling down on me. I feel like I am under the earth, underground, like in a coal mine. The earth is shaking with dirt and stones falling. The tunnel is collapsing. There is dust, and I am gasping for breath. I don't think I am getting out of it.*

After expressing words of support and safety, I ask Rob if he died.

*I don't feel any different. But I am scared, scared of the nothing-ness. The nothingness is claustrophobic, awful. I feel panic wondering how to get out of here. It is like a hell, this overwhelming nothingness.*

47

*I feel alone. I can't imagine anyone being here. There is nothing but nothingness here.*

Souls' intentions play out. The power behind the past life decision to never be overpowered is fueled by fear. Rob is focusing on what he does not want, on his fear of being crushed. We create what we fear. After his death, Rob is experiencing his deepest fear.

When clients experience a sense of nothingness and isolation, I usually ask if they find anything positive about that state. When I ask this of Rob, he gives me the answer I have heard so many times before. He says he feels safe here. He doesn't like being used by others, and here he is alone. When I ask if there is anyone he can trust, he names another miner called John. John used to take him for a drink in the pub at the end of their shift.

I realize John must have died many years ago and his spirit might have moved on, but I also know that Linda's spirit guides have taken us to this past life to resolve the past trauma. I am confident that somehow John will appear, so I ask Rob if he would accept an invitation from John.

*I just got a sense of someone with red hair. It's John! It's vague but I sense he is smiling. I am numb. Shocked. The change in circumstances was so unexpected. John is taking me somewhere. I see green fields and a stream. I am happy here. [Crying.] I am glad to be out of the darkness. I feel relieved. I am washing all the dirt off me in the stream. Now I am sitting in the sun. Oh! I see a group of miners who died in the mine too. They are saying "It is okay now. We are out of that mine." I am happy to be out of it.*

Although Rob wasn't close to people, he was generous and respected by the community. People who need to feel in control of their relationships are often generous. Giving rather than receiving provides a sense of control and safety. Reciprocity is a common pattern, deeply held in the human psyche. When we accept a gift or help from others, we feel an underlying tension that remains until we reciprocate in some way. Generosity helps us feel safe because we sense the other owes us and is less likely to do us harm.

Linda's soul became lost after she decided to never be overpowered again. This decision imprinted the soul and played out in subsequent lifetimes in various ways. Rob wasn't overpowered by people in his life, but he was overwhelmed by the mine collapsing and becoming lost in nothingness after his death. His spirit remained trapped until he was freed by Linda during the regression.

## Overreacting: A Clue to the Past

Accessing a past life means bringing forgotten experiences into the present. During a regression, there is a rich interplay between the person we are now—our personality, the beliefs we hold, our current emotional state—and the person we were in that past life. We are different people, but unresolved experiences from our past lives still influence our current lives. Once our past life traumas are resolved, they no longer have a hold over us. If we are still haunted by traumatic lives, we can be negative, closed down, guilt ridden, or full of blame. If we have resolved some past life trauma while other traumas still remain, we may vacillate between joy and negativity depending on our current circumstances. When we live in the shadow of past life trauma, seemingly innocuous experiences can trigger us, bringing our past into the present.

Todd, a teacher, was under the care of a doctor, psychiatrist, and psychologist, each greatly concerned with his state of mind and his suicide attempts. Over a span of three years, Todd came to see me three times. After reviewing the notes of these sessions, I realized his suffering was a culmination of pain accumulated over several lifetimes. This was also evident from a statement he made in his first session.

*I am fulfilling a purpose that goes over a number of lifetimes. It is a big project, and I won't finish it this lifetime.*

Todd is gradually releasing his underlying sense of being flawed. In spite of his innocence in a past life and his current life, he has been unable to free himself of this sense of inadequacy that plagues him.

Two years before our first session, a disengaged, hostile student had falsely accused Todd of hitting him. Todd's reaction to this libel was disproportionate. His headmaster referred the matter to the police, and even though the investigation that followed cleared him of any wrongdoing, Todd remained angry, devastated, depressed, and suicidal. In desperation, he resigned from his teaching position. Before he came for his first session, he still suffered from depression, anxiety, and suicidal ideation.

During the regression, Todd accessed a past life as a very young girl falsely charged with witchcraft. Although she protests her innocence, the elders of the village decide to conduct a trial by water. She is bound and thrown into a river. If she sinks, she will be deemed innocent and pulled out. If she floats, she will be condemned as guilty. Todd reports what happens.

*My hands are tied. I am up on the surface. [Pause.] Now I am going down, deeper and deeper. I don't want them to kill me and believe I was guilty. I am determined to prove my innocence.*

In reality, the young girl dies, but from her perspective she is still fighting to prove her innocence. Thus, she never accepts her death. Instead, her sense of injustice and her vow to survive trap her spirit in a timeless struggle for survival and absolution.

Being falsely accused at the school triggered Todd's unresolved trauma from this past life. I ask him if he can see any link between the past life and the present.

*The headmaster had me trapped, and I had no way to escape. I can see I was resonating with this past injustice. I can feel how determined the drowning girl was to prove them wrong. She desperately wanted to survive.*

So desperate to be proven innocent, the young girl failed to realize that proof is not really required when you know, in the depths of your soul, that you have done nothing wrong. As she sank down into the water, she sensed her guilt, shame, and worthlessness, accumulated from previous past lives. These feelings had surfaced in Todd again when the student bore false witness against him. He, too, was desperate to clear his name.

Todd values being strong-willed but wants to know how to let go of his old fears. I tell Todd that even though the young girl yearned to survive, she drowned in front of the villagers. Now is the time to come to terms with her loss. Todd takes one slow, deep breath, then finds himself back in the water.

Todd's body is shaking all over. I encourage him to keep breathing, slow and steady. He faces the harsh truth that the young girl died unfairly, drawing her feelings of disappointment into his heart. Only when he has fully embraced those feelings can he gradually let go of her life.

*Now I am in a field of flowers. My guides are here, telling me they are proud of me. It feels good.*

Rescuing the young girl from her watery grave gave Todd some relief, and his medical professionals were surprised by his sudden improvement. But three years later he returned to see me, still struggling with suicidal ideation.

Sadly, his medical practitioners could only offer him limited help. He told me they panic when he shares his desperation and suicidal thoughts, which only isolates him more. They do not understand that he is suffering an existential crisis that will take several lifetimes to resolve.

As we have seen, profound experiences in one life can impact our later lives. When an event occurs in our current life that is similar to the trauma in the past life, it triggers the original reaction.

Post-traumatic stress, or PTSD, is the same. A serious event like a car accident, a sudden loss, or anything that causes a deep shock can shake us to the core. The emotional charge and imprinted memories of the trauma can stay with us and later trigger a reaction. If you ever find yourself overreacting to something another person says or does, perhaps you are still carrying some PTSD from old wounds. Being triggered tells you this trauma remains unresolved. The emotion that fuels your overreaction may come from trauma you experienced earlier in your current life, in a past life, or both.

## Slipping Down

Avoiding the pain of trauma is a strategy with limited efficacy. By getting angry and isolating, we can evade our present suffering, but our wounds are not healed, and our past will continue to stalk us.

Nora came for a regression with a number of issues, including relationship problems, claustrophobia, and back pain. During the regression, she visited several past lives. In one she is an aunt looking after her deceased brother's children. She loves the children but doesn't care for their mother, whom she describes as unstable.

*I can see some children who are sick and dying. I try to help them with some medicine. I feel completely desperate. I give them medicine, herbs I have picked. There is nothing more I can do to save them.*

*The priest comes. He is with the children when they are dying. Everyone is confused about what happened. Someone says they were poisoned. Now I am not sure if they were sick or poisoned. The widow and the rest of the family are pointing the finger at me.*

*I have to turn around and run. I try to hide at a friend's place. I can feel the panic. I am in agony, despair, and misery. I am stuck right now. I am hiding. There is nowhere else to go. I know I will hang. I feel very scared.*

*They are going to hang me. I am angry. Very angry. I want revenge. I am making a curse. I will get her [the widow] in another life.*

Nora was hanged for something she believes she didn't do. She turned away from Source and invoked a diabolical power to avenge her death.

A curse is the opposite of atonement (at-one-ment). Hating someone and seeking revenge separates us from Source. It affects the soul. As we saw in the previous chapter, we are all ultimately "one." At a fundamental level, a curse on others is a curse on ourselves. If we believe our curses have the power to hurt others, it follows that we believe others' curses have the power to harm us. We find ourselves living in a menacing occult world.

Nora's subsequent life shows how her act of separation plays out. In this life, she is a strongly built fisherman, who loves nothing more than being out on the sea fishing. Although he has a wife and two children, he likes being alone.

*I am not at home often, and I can't think of where I live because it is not important. I am not a good family man. It all feels a bit pointless.*

*I look at the children and I am scared. I am afraid something will happen to them. I feel anxiety, no control. I want to run away from the feeling. When I am away, I don't feel that so much. I am terrified of my own children. I wasn't prepared for those feelings when I had those children.*

*It is my job to be a fisherman, and I use it as my excuse to be out at sea. It is so peaceful. I don't want to go home. I stay out late. I feel like I ended up never going home. I stayed out on the boat and abandoned my family. I let them drift away. I live on my boat and go into other ports.*

The fisherman cannot emotionally connect with his family. He is now living in the menacing world inadvertently created by soul choices made in previous lives. The aunt whose nephews and nieces died felt powerless. She couldn't save the children, nor could she save herself. She felt victimized by the rest of her family and couldn't accept what happened. She resorted to anger, disconnecting from Source and seeking revenge.

Her lack of trust passed on to the fisherman. He avoids responsibility and caring for his family, believing that distance will protect him from the pain of losing them. This is a strategy many souls use after experiencing a deep hurt in a life where they felt overly responsible.

Nora receives some insight into these two past lives.

*I ignored how my actions affected others, and that can be selfish. I think short-term rather than long-term, especially in relationships. I ignore those relationships with people I don't care about or who are difficult. I dismiss the ones who are difficult to deal with.*

*As the fisherman, I was scared of caring for the children, of damaging them in some way and of being hurt. I didn't trust myself. I wanted to love but I didn't know how to do it safely.*

*In my current life, I have chosen not to have children. The fisherman had an opportunity to do it right and he didn't. I haven't forgiven him. I feel like I can only live my lives with minimum responsibility.*

*I need to pay more attention to people, realize their needs are important, and look at what they need. All the problems I have with my back are from that life. I have the feeling that no one has my back. I run away because I don't trust myself.*

*My widowed sister-in-law is my mother in my current life. I felt so angry with my mother and I never understood why. I would think about pushing her down the stairs. I am hitting "cancel, clear, delete" to the curse I put on her when I was on the scaffold.*

Nora blamed the fisherman for her decision not to have a family in her current life. She didn't understand why the fisherman chose to isolate and hadn't taken full responsibility for her decision to remain childless.

Her back pain is one issue she wishes to address. I suggest she go to the origin of the problem. Nora finds herself in an enclosed space. We discover she is experiencing a past life as a reckless man. He was engaged to marry but got tangled up with another woman, sabotaging his marriage plans and shortening his life.

*I feel like I am in a box, a punishment box. There are two holes, and I am looking outside. I can see some trees.*

*Someone in authority didn't like me and left me there. I feel like I am there forever. I cannot stand up, but I cannot sit down either. I feel very uncomfortable, and my back is feeling very bad. I feel so hopeless and sad.*

I make suggestions to help Nora free this trapped spirit. Gradually, he realizes he died in the box and doesn't need to be trapped there anymore. He goes to the light. Now Nora gains more information about that life.

*That life ended much earlier than expected. From that experience, I lost trust and my soul got damaged. The life feels like a waste. But it is not a waste if I use it to remind me to not rush. That life and death made me a very determined person, more focused and serious about things. I was better at seeing what is important.*

Decisions made in Nora's previous lives did not solve her problems. In seeking to avoid more pain, she ended up taking a wrong turn. She drew no long-term comfort from calling on diabolical powers to damn her sister-in-law. With this curse, she abandoned her true self, those close to her, and her connection to Source. The fisherman couldn't settle and spent his life alone, troubled by the guilt of failing his family. The reckless man was afraid to commit to his fiancée, and his infidelity cost him dearly. Being trapped in the box after death had a purpose. Nora's soul carried a subconscious memory of the consequences of being reckless and impulsive, which manifested as physical pain in her back. Now that she knows how she created her back pain, she can use it as a signal to correct her actions, take responsibility in her relationships, and be more aware of the needs of others.

Nora's lives demonstrate how our decisions have consequences that reverberate in subsequent lifetimes. Trying to avoid pain just takes us deeper into distress. We need to face, acknowledge, and work through our heartache and loss if we don't want to slide into a path of more misery and turmoil.

## Imprints Are Created During Incarnations

Some people wonder why we don't make changes when we are in between our lives. Behavioral patterns and beliefs formed during our physical lives are imprinted at the earth level of vibration. When we want to change our views, we need to do so consciously in a physical body rather than just doing so energetically. Healing these patterns while we are incarnated imprints the change more robustly because we are connected to both physical and nonphysical worlds. Making positive changes while in the body deeply imprints the soul memory.

Some clients find that their current lives have been created specifically to change patterns that were imprinted during previous lives. Evaline is one of these people. Evaline experienced a life thousands of years ago when a catastrophic explosion occurred, destroying much of the earth and inundating what remained with devastating floods.

*I just keep seeing the explosion over and over again. I get the same feeling I get when I visualize the future environment of our current world. This feeling has come from this [past life] explosion. I foresaw this coming, and it was a serious, huge devastation. I tried to warn the hierarchy, but they didn't listen. It set up a chain reaction on the planet. Some did survive but not many. I didn't survive.*

Spirit guides take Evaline through a process that heals her trauma from this past life, which includes beautiful visions and peaceful feelings. She receives the message to focus on her inner serenity and not worry about the bigger picture of the planet.

Before she came for the regression, Evaline wanted to know her purpose in this life. She learns that her *only* purpose for her current life is to heal certain patterns of behavior, which were imprinted during numerous previous lives. In fact, her current life had been created specifically to heal these patterns.

## The Benefit of Being Lost

We have seen how becoming lost can impact our future lives in a way that takes us deeper down a path of struggle and suffering. We can also carry over memories that are useful.

Gayle, a public servant, is a self-confident, pleasant lady who lives alone and loves animals. After I have instructed her to go through a tunnel into a past life, she reports what she sees.

*It is daytime, and I am outside looking at the front of a house. It is bigger than a cottage and the walls are made of stone, sealed with mortar. It has a grey roof and a path leading to an ordinary timber door. I have no strong feelings about this place. I am an outsider.*

*I am an older woman with old legs, wearing comfortable black leather shoes and a knee-length skirt. I am eighty-three years old, and it is the early twentieth century.*

*I am walking along the path to the door, which has blue trimming. I feel I am entitled to open the door. It is cold inside. I see lace curtains, linoleum floors, a heavy round table, and old horsehair couches. There is nothing expensive here. The house is empty. People lived here once, but no one lives here now. There is an old parlor, but it is not inviting.*

I ask if she has lived in this house. Her answer is instant and unexpected.

*I died in a bed upstairs. Oh! I only just realized. I must be dead. I hadn't known that before. I died without realizing I was dead. I am downstairs looking up the stairs to the room where my body was. I am detached from any emotions.*

She says her name in this life had been Ruby and, looking back, describes what Ruby was like.

*When I was alive, I was a quiet person with no strong emotions and not many friends. It was not an exciting life. I lived within the conventions of the time. I didn't need to be strongly expressive and I accepted that. Now I realize there was some emptiness in my life. It was the era. I was a spinster living here, as it was the family home. I didn't change it. It was a bland life.*

*I am hanging around. I had religious beliefs, but not to any depth. I just accepted things as they were.*

I ask her what she is going to do now that she knows she died.

*I feel a need to go out onto the road and walk on. I need to let go of the house, to let go of the life. That is a funny experience. It makes me see how much one can attach to walls, beds, stairs, and tables. That was all that I knew.*

*I am going out the door and closing it, walking down the cement path, out the gate, and heading off down the road. I feel that was the right thing to do. It feels good. Sunlight is coming through the trees. I don't feel old anymore. There is energy in my step, and I feel younger and happy.*

*I am walking along pleasantly and enjoying the freedom. I see there is light up ahead, a strong light. I am very drawn to it. Someone is there with light all around them.*

I suggest she open herself up so she can connect to this light and receive any forthcoming information.

*I am in an expanding aura of light and it feels very warm. I need to stand and let it infuse me so I can go on. It has made me feel free. It is like it has dusted out the corners, cleared out anything unwanted from that life, realigned me, and retuned my vibration so I can now transition.*

After walking along another path, she comes to a building made of marble.

*There are people in there, older men. I am going in. They are very quiet, sitting around in chairs. They have been waiting for me.*

*They tell me that past life was about loving others, but Ruby was unable to step outside of the social structure. She was restricted. The plan was to have courage and break through.*

*I chose to stay in that house and restrict my life. It was about feeling safe. There was no depth to relationships or anything. Everything was a bit superficial and I was able to hide behind the social norms. I was afraid.*

*The church, the fire and brimstone. I believed it. One had to do one's duty. The church triggered my fear and insecurity, then fed it.*

*I was a young child, about three, and something scared me. I see a minister from the church. He was very harsh with me. Oh my God!*

*They were my parents. My father was the minister, and he was yelling at me. I lived in that house all my life, and the way I lived my life was related to the way he frightened me at age three. It was an obstacle put in my way, but I didn't overcome it and I didn't expand my heart.*

I ask if Ruby's life has influenced her current life as Gayle. Gayle was bullied terribly in her current life as a child, but in adulthood would not stand for any bullying at all. Gayle moves her focus to her current life.

*That is why I was so determined not to let the bullies keep me down. I have a sense of it now. Even when I was being bullied as a child, I knew I was going to stop that as soon as I could. I had that determination even then.*

Gayle continues but describes Ruby's experiences in the third person when I ask if Ruby was lost until now.

*Yes. Even in life, Ruby was not functioning fully, just going through the motions—detached, but not in a good way.*

*For Ruby, being stuck after she died emphasized the hollowness of her life. Now I don't need it anymore. Going through that purification with the light-being means it is finished.*

*Isn't that amazing! That life gave me the understanding that if you let fear govern you, there is emptiness, narrowness, and no expansion. A hollow life. That understanding evolved from that past life. It was just there. After eighty years of that, I knew how empty your life would be if you did not address it. Ruby's life was meant to be. Such a dull life but such a useful life. It wasn't a waste.*

*In my current life, when a bully has tried to manipulate me, I will not buy into it. Others do, but not me. I attack bullies full on. As I have matured, I can look at a bully and see that they came from a place of imbalance.*

Gayle's case demonstrates how being lost can accelerate our growth. Ruby was lost during her life and after her death, feeling that her father's bullying had driven her to live a small, confined life. This feeling was made available to Gayle in her current life, and she used it to develop an inner strength, refusing to put up with bullies.

## Conclusion

Being lost can take us deeper into strife and suffering. But if we stay connected, we can decide to utilize a troubled past life to make us stronger.

We start our lives as innocent babies, but we do not stay that way. In our current lives, we face challenges that surface subconscious memories of the past. Because we carry the energy of lost spirits, our reaction to some situations can be much more intense than is normally warranted. Our most vigorous and extreme reactions are worth noting. Some trauma from the past may have been triggered, manifesting in our current life. When a human spirit doesn't go home after death, the energy of that life remains unresolved and still accessible.

The emotional trauma we carry into subsequent lives demands our attention. This is why many of my clients remember lives in which they died suddenly—because such lives have so much to teach us. If we refuse to listen when past life traumas flare up in our current life, we condemn ourselves to keep playing out our adopted patterns of behavior until we finally wake up.

In the next three chapters, we explore the journeys of four souls who did decide to step bravely into their dark night of the soul.

# SECTION 2:
# INTO THE DEPTHS

# CHAPTER 3
# AGREEING TO BE
# THE PERPETRATOR

Souls have free will. We agree to incarnate on earth with all that entails. We may become lost, confused, victimized, or villainous. But we make our decision without realizing how deeply immersive our experiences on earth shall be. This ignorance is a major attraction of this dense planet. Coming here is an adventure. Just as some of us want to try all the games and rides at a theme park, including the scary ones, some souls want to try all the experiences earth offers.

We do not play perpetrator roles without our agreement. We might be chosen rather than volunteering, but our agreement is still needed. To fully experience the earth, we need to know what it is like to be cut off from Source and go it alone. We plan experiences that lure us down this track of isolation. Anyone venturing into unknown territory all alone will build courage and inner strength. This is a process of individuation and part of the earth curriculum.

Ultimately, at the highest levels of understanding, no actions are good or bad. They are seen just as experiences. But that doesn't feel true to us here on earth. Although a few people glorify war and cruelty, most of us do not. We abhor it, desiring peace, love, acceptance, and respect. But have you noticed the dilemma in the previous statement? Hating the actions of the haters puts us all in the same negative category. How can we reconcile this contradiction?

We need boundaries on earth. We want our freedom, but we also want to be protected. We have laws, rules, and customs. When we break the law, we are rightly punished. When we disrespect others, we are chastised. The consequences we reap are important teachers.

We can censure those who cross boundaries while understanding why and how they transgressed. Understanding is not the same as excusing.

I was challenged to make this distinction with Yvette, a lovely client I knew from my psychology practice. She was the first of my clients who relived a past life as a cruel perpetrator. You might remember Yvette, whose case I mentioned in the introduction. In this chapter we follow her story, exploring the preamble to the slave trader's life, how the slave trader turned around, and the struggle back to reconnecting to Source.

## The Slave Trader

Yvette found she was repeatedly attracted to narcissists. She wanted to know why she had this unwitting attraction and how she could avoid this trap.

What is a narcissist? The mythological Narcissus could not love others. He spurned them. Instead, he fell in love with the superficial vision of himself. People with narcissistic personality disorder are characterized as being arrogant, lacking in empathy, needing excessive admiration, oppressing others, and carrying a sense of entitlement.

In Yvette's regression, we discovered she had been a narcissistic slave trader in a past life. Now we return to Yvette's regression to understand how she came to be a cold-hearted slave trader—

and how this past life had been influencing her choices in her current life.

The slave trader lived a long time ago in a town on the Arabian Peninsula. He sold a young slave girl to a lascivious old man. At first, the slave trader enjoyed the thought of her suffering at the hands of this man, but his enjoyment didn't last. The girl stared at him, not with despair but with disgust. Yvette, as the slave trader, describes what happens next.

*I start having nightmares about the slave girl, and this is the beginning of me going mad.*

*I have a wife and children, including a little girl of three. My daughter loves me so much. She adores me and looks up to me. I wonder what she would think about the work I do.*

*I cannot stop selling people because of the money. Life is hard without money. You are in the good class or the bad class and I want to stay in the good class. So I keep doing it and suffering the nightmares. I continually see the eyes of the young slave girl burning into me. Even though she was frightened, she looked at me with pity as if she was saying, "How can you do this?" In my dreams, her eyes go right through me and her face transforms horribly, haunting me.*

*I am not coping well in the market. I argue about the price of a slave with a man who loses his temper. He stabs me with a knife. His eyes are the same as the girl's, looking at me with pity.*

*I am dying. I feel sad to leave my family but also relieved it is over. I was in turmoil.*

## Freeing the Slave Trader

As the slave trader passes over, I notice Yvette is quiet. I assume she is processing the information that is coming through. Eventually, she breaks the silence.

*I feel warmth and love. Someone is coming to greet me, saying, "We have been waiting for you." Oh! I see the same eyes of the young slave girl I sold on earth. She is one of my soulmates. She is looking at me with such love.*

*How crazy! Does this normally happen? I cannot believe that these words are coming out of my mouth. I just know she was that girl and I was that man who sold people.*

Yvette is embraced by the former slave. I pause to allow her to absorb the love, but she is struggling. The heart of the slave trader had been closed for a long time. Yvette feels a lot of pain in her heart, and I encourage her to embrace and breathe through the pain to soften the hardness.

Fifteen minutes later, the pain subsides. We discover that slave trading was an occupation passed down from previous generations. The slave trader's father taught him to be ruthless by beating him brutally, just as he had been beaten by his own father. Slave traders have to be cold and hard. The young boy learns his lessons well, passing on his pain to others, including animals and his little brother.

*I become hard. Why would I care about the slaves? I have never been happy. When I see them suffer, I feel something inside, a sort of pleasure that fills a void. The only thing I treasure is my daughter. She is my only joy, the only real feeling I have.*

The slave trader disconnects from his true self, from others, and from Source. Feeling isolated, he is numb and empty inside, focusing on survival and material wealth. His daughter and the slave girl are the only ones who can crack his shell of isolation.

The slave trader's life began the process of breaking the pattern of disconnection, which his soul had been playing out. Two soulmates volunteered to help: his daughter and the slave girl. Although this life was a turning point, this soul was not clear after the slave trader's death. There was a long way back to reconnect to the greater self.

## Sympathy for Narcissists

The conflict and confusion of the slave trader experienced at his death was triggered in Yvette's current life. It may have been present in other lives too. She felt sympathy for narcissists, especially those who felt alone and lost. This accounted for her attraction to these unsuitable men whom she tried to help. She was too clouded to assess them accurately. As we will see, she only obtained full clarity when she accessed her life between lives during the regression, when the full story of her dark night of the soul was revealed.

## The Pact: Never Again

After Yvette recounts the slave trader's death, I wonder why she experienced this life as a perpetrator. Was the slave trader's contempt just the result of his childhood? Or was there more to the story? I ask for more information.

Yvette is taken to a past life that occurred two thousand years before the slave trader was born.

*I am in South America, living as part of a native group in the Amazonian forest. I am a young girl playing with other children. We feel free and wear very little. We are all having fun, dancing around the fire. We live in harmony and are happy.*

*Another group, with people who look like us, is coming. They have more clothes and more weapons than we do. They are using wooden spears and axes to kill all the old people. They take us away. We walk and walk and walk. They are ritually sacrificing the men, and I am being sold because I am a girl.*

*I am sold to a wealthy family. I am a servant and sexual object for the father and his son. Every time they sexually assault me, I kill a part of my soul. I don't want to feel the pain anymore, so I surrender to the darkness. I am empty. I make a survival pact. I will never let anyone hurt me again. I die from sickness, aged fifteen.*

*The pact means I will hurt others rather than be hurt. When I go up, I am lost. I can see someone waiting for me, but I am so angry I push them away, saying, "How can you let this happen to me?"*

As we have seen in the previous chapter, making a pact to never allow herself to be hurt will take Yvette down a perilous path.

## Lost In Between Heaven and Earth

After this life of forced servitude, the young girl's soul refuses to go home with her guide because of her anger and bitterness. She describes where she is.

*I am in between—in between earth and heaven. I feel alone, but there are other people around who are like me. It is such a weird place. All this lost energy. Everybody seems lost. Some know they need to go up, but they don't understand why they cannot. Others don't even realize that they are supposed to go up. For me, I just don't care. Because they [the higher beings] let me suffer so terribly, why would they help anybody? If we are love, why would they let some of us suffer so much? Why do we have to come back to earth and have this physical experience that is so painful? It is safer in the darkness because you already know what to expect. It is less painful because it is empty.*

As we have seen in the previous chapter, Yvette's explanation of preferring emptiness to being on earth is not new. We encountered spirits who found themselves in a cold place of emptiness and darkness.

# Perpetrator and Victim Lives

I ask Yvette how she got out of this dark, empty state.

*Someone comes to me in that place, saying, "You start to see, Little One. Remember the Source when you were first born as a soul?"*

*I remembered, and it felt beautiful, better than being lost. I just get a taste of it. I have to go back to have earthly lives and work on opening up. I am not ready to get it yet. I have to keep working on it. I agree to play the perpetrator. The guides say to me, "If that is what you want, Little One, you can go back to earth and do that. Be a perpetrator."*

*I had three or four lifetimes as a perpetrator. The first one was the worst, the most violent. I can see I am torturing people.*

After those perpetrator lives, which included the slave trader life, Yvette had many other lives, some as a victim. She describes one of these lives, which she experienced during the regression.

*I am walking along the corridor of a castle with portraits on the walls in medieval times. I am fifteen, wearing a blue dress, beautiful but simple, made of natural fabric. My blonde hair is braided and wrapped around my head. Looking at the portraits, I feel a lot of anger, frustration, and jealousy. I want to belong, but the people here are mean to me. In my heart I am supposed to belong, but I don't.*

*It hurts. I am confused because I don't understand why people are so cruel and mean to me.*

*I am in an old kitchen with a big oven cut in the stone walls. People are working there, and one of the cooks is telling me the nobleman and his family will never love me. I am not accepted as one of his family because even though I am his daughter, the cook is my mother. I have his eyes. The others are mean and jealous because the nobleman is kind to me. I think he really loves my mother, but they are not from the same world.*

71

The young girl is distraught. She feels the rejection of her father and the family deeply. She suddenly jumps out of a high castle opening, dying.

*I can see my father is very sad, crying over my body. Soon after I died, my mother sickened and died too.*

*My heart hurts. I couldn't help this girl. I recognize the pain of this life, the feeling of not belonging and the self-loathing. She was fifteen.*

*In my current life, I tried to kill myself at fifteen. It was when my mother cut me off, punishing me because I wanted to live with my father.*

A familiar pattern has played out in many of Yvette's feminine lives—trauma, followed by death at the age of fifteen. As a young girl forced into domestic and sexual slavery, she became ill and died at fifteen. After that experience, she chose to incarnate as a perpetrator. In this medieval life, she commits suicide at fifteen. In her current life, she tried to kill herself at fifteen but failed. This failure began to break the pattern.

I have had other clients who have similar patterns run through their past lives. One client relived two lives where she died at sixteen and nearly did the same again in her current life. According to her guide, she was naïve and reckless, and he successfully helped her avoid the same fate.

## Reaching Home

Yvette's medieval past life is one of the many lives she undertakes on her way back to love. After throwing herself from the window, she arrives at her life between lives. She is surrounded by her soul group.

*They are saying, "You are now ready to start the next chapter." Wow!*

*There are other souls here who I know. We are together, and there is no judgment. We don't even need to speak. We communicate so easily and understand each other so well. I have a strong sense of belonging and connection.*

*I am part of a soul group, and we are only as strong as all of us. Soulmates cannot turn their back on the lost one. Love conquers all. Light conquers all. They love me unconditionally.*

*Part of my soul journey is the betterment of the whole soul group. They tell me that one day I will be ready to come back as love. I am not to be afraid anymore. Now they are asking me what I am going to do now that I know all of this.*

*I am a leader, and I am not to doubt what I feel. I can see the impact of my current life's childhood. I was lost. I had a pull to do something about it. Because I had not dealt with it, I wasn't grounded in my body. Because of all the therapy I have undertaken during my life, I am better grounded now and done with the past.*

Yvette has been carrying the guilt of the slave trader over many incarnations. This helped her stay on the path of reaching for the light. Now, that guilt has been released. She has developed a deep, firsthand understanding of perpetrators and victims, how they fall down, and how they ascend. This gives her a depth of compassion that can be used to help others.

*What I have been feeling is the right path for me. My mission is to help traumatized children become grounded, especially those in their teenage years who have struggled like I did. Even though each one has a different, specific struggle, all follow a similar pattern and direction. I am to help these teens connect with their real self.*

*If you can do all these awful things and recover, you can help others. Love is always within you, not outside of you. It never left you. I am to help these teens understand that love is always within.*

Yvette shared earlier in her session with me that she senses spirits visiting her at night, alarming her. Now she is beginning to understand what has been going on.

*My soulmates are telling me not to be afraid of the lost ones who come to see me at night. I am to help them too. These are people who have died and are stuck. They don't remember who they are. But I know who they are. I was like them. I know what it is like to be lost. The guides are saying, "Thank you for helping out, Little One."*

Yvette returns from her life between lives feeling light and energized. She is amazed to learn how lost she was, but now all her guilt and pity has dissipated.

Eighteen months later, she writes to tell me how her life has changed. After the regression, she was never attracted to a narcissist again.

*Everything has been going very fast, actually. I guess this is what happens when you remember who you are. I have embraced myself fully and discovered a self-love that I never knew could exist. I feel so grateful for it and have been on this amazing life journey full of love and experience. My third eye and connection to spirits has been stronger than ever. I have met and connected with wonderful people along the way, and it is not over. This fills me with so much joy. The challenges of life don't feel so hard anymore, just a question of perspective.*

Yvette's soul chose to take the perpetrator path long ago after a brief life filled with extreme suffering. By default, her iron-clad decision to never suffer again sent her into a state of suspended darkness for hundreds of years. After she emerged from her protective cocoon, she decided to undertake lives as perpetrators. She wasn't ready to trust again. She still felt bruised and unwilling to open up her heart, which would involve being vulnerable and hurt. By default, a soul's decision to never be hurt is a choice of separation. Playing perpetrator roles kept her heart closed. That felt safer.

After four lives as a perpetrator, her soul was ready for the change. The slave trader life was a turning point. It began the reversal of her earlier decision to never suffer again. The guilt from the slave trader's life carried over into her subsequent lives. Carried-over guilt is useful, reminding her to avoid perpetrating against others. At this stage, she had not fully opened up her heart, being still afraid and self-protective. But her fear of being hurt creates what she dreads most: terrible emotional pain, like the rejection she experienced as the illegitimate daughter of a nobleman. But her lives of suffering are useful. She learns what it is like to be victimized, the flip side of perpetration. This crystalizes her desire to never willingly make anyone suffer in the future.

Remnants of guilt were left over from the slave trader life and the medieval life, but they had a purpose. These energies bled into her current life, causing her problems and giving her an opportunity to awaken. She set out on the path of discovering who she really was. She succeeded, healing the past life remnants while gaining a deeper understanding of her true self.

Yvette's soul has experienced many heavy lives as a perpetrator and a victim, but these no longer define her. She is connected to her true self and sees ahead a path of service, utilizing the knowledge and wisdom she has developed. She is proceeding down this path with much joy and a new partner who is kind, loving, and committed to spending his life with her.

## Conclusion

We might wonder why we are attracted to someone, especially when the person turns out to be unsuitable. When the same unwanted pattern of attraction keeps happening, we may be compelled to go searching for the reasons, as Yvette did. This is wise.

We can be confused when our choice of partner or friends do not work out as we expected. Our choices are not random or accidental. There are reasons for our emotional responses and actions, but our deeper motivations are not always apparent.

We need to dig deep to discover why we are falling into the same patterns. Probably, it involves some unique past experience that remains unresolved. Humans are complex, and our experiences are unique and many. What we find is not likely to be as disturbing or unexpected as what Yvette discovered. But whatever lies beneath, spending our time and energy in the quest to bring it to the light is worthwhile. Once we gain a full understanding of what has happened, we are liberated from our unhealthy attractions and compulsions.

## CHAPTER 4
# DESCENT INTO ASSAULT AND TORTURE

People who assault and torture others have souls that have strayed into the wilderness. They have suffered in the past and decided to trust no one. This means they are on their own, making their way in a world they see as dark and dangerous. Cut off from their inner wisdom and cut off from other people, they are ignorant of the feelings of others. In fact, they are so detached, their ability to understand or predict the actions of others is greatly compromised. A path not lit by the wisdom of higher guidance will always prove dark. In lifetime after lifetime, they stumble around in the shadows, creating turmoil and destruction for themselves and others until they learn that this path is a dead end.

In this chapter we explore the limitations of souls in this state, their fear and vigilance, shame, eventual awakening, and the climb back to connection and understanding.

## Blind to the Motivations of Others

Souls that are not aware of their own motivations are lost, not knowing what they are doing or the consequences of their behavior. They are blind to the relationship between their actions and their experiences. As well, their failure to understand themselves means they cannot understand or predict the behavior of others.

Hayden was a lost soul in several of his past lives. In one past life, he was a giant of a man who was troubled from the beginning.

He enjoyed torturing animals during his childhood. But then something happened that made him even worse: his mother died while he was still a boy. His father, full of grief, took him into the forest and left him standing alone on a road. Although he said he'd be back, he never returned. The boy perceived his father as weak because he never got over the loss of his wife. He despised his father's vulnerability. He coped with this abandonment by deciding he needed no one. Now we move to a later time in this life as Hayden continues the story.

*Now the child is a man. People are looking for him. He believes he can outrun them, thinking he is smarter than them. He has been killing people randomly. He despises vulnerability. He hurts them until they don't hurt anymore, until they are dead. He enjoys watching the fear on people's faces. He thought he could make them fear him, but they hunt him like an animal. He could never understand why they were so determined. He didn't expect that. He thought they would leave him alone. He still doesn't understand. He is confused.*

The man is subjected to a tortuous death in front of the men from the village where he took his victims. He hated these people, thinking they were weak and foolish. He wanted to be alone, and he thought they would be too afraid to come after him. He never realized that his vicious behavior would cultivate enormous anger and hate, which he would eventually reap. By his actions, he had created in the villagers an angry, vengeful version of himself.

Souls like this man's are not self-aware or self-reflective. They cannot be. They are too wrapped up in satisfying their own need to stay safe in the menacing world they have mentally created. They are on constant alert, afraid of others who they perceive as dangerous. In this case, the man was so apprehensive, he attacked without provocation.

To reflect, make connections, and understand ourselves, the world, and others, we need to feel safe. We need to calm our mind. None of this is possible for perpetrators or perpetual victims. The world is too dangerous for them to let their guard down—even for a minute—to undertake insightful contemplation.

Climbing out of this deep darkness is not easy. First, we have to waken to what we have done, then understand completely the terrible actions we have taken by suffering torture and abuse ourselves. Lastly, we have to find a way to universal forgiveness and redemption.

## Facing Shame

An example of this long, challenging journey comes from a client who came for six regressions over a period of three years. Terry, a builder, is one of the most courageous people I know. He is on the hero's journey of facing his demons. Most people think their demons are outside of themselves, like the horrific monsters we see in comics and movies. Terry knows the real demons are inside us.

Terry had resolved many of his issues before he came for his most recent regression. Most importantly, the anger he described as "bubbling lava" had been put to rest. Now, he decided to face his deepest shame. He acknowledged this was difficult, but he had gained sufficient success and confidence from our previous sessions to trust that I would not judge him in any way.

In the session, once he had settled comfortably in the chair, he proceeded to tell me about the burden he had been carrying all his life.

*I feel like I am a sexual predator. I have always wanted to see up girls' skirts and into their pants. As a small boy, the babysitter would put me and her daughter in the bath together, and I remember being curious and fascinated by her little body. From my earliest memories, the compulsion has been there, and that's why I think it has carried over from a past life.*

*It is a daily battle to keep my eyes up. I haven't acted on these urges. There has been something driving me down that path all my life, and I have continually fought it. I am so tired of every day facing the urge and the shame of it. It has been a lonely battle. I never shared it with anyone, including my wonderful wife who I love dearly.*

## Hate and Sexual Assault

Terry's story starts many thousands of years ago when he first incarnated on the planet.

His first human life occurred 27,000 years ago when he died, aged two, of the cold. After that life, he had many simple lives that were mainly peaceful. He only behaved aggressively when he needed to protect his family or community.

These ordinary lives changed significantly around 10 BCE, during a life set in a rural area of the Iberian Peninsula. Before this incarnation, Terry experienced a life where he was betrayed. We don't learn any details of this betrayal, but his guide tells us it was relatively inconsequential. Perhaps Terry still carried some bitterness into the Iberian life, because there he makes a devastating decision.

*It is dusk. I am looking out onto open plains with a village behind me. I am dressed in soft leather shoes, leather or suede long pants and a long-sleeve shirt with no buttons. All are an olive color. I am a man aged twenty-four.*

*The village is made of huts set out in a horseshoe shape. Each hut is made of leather with a conical roof held up by a high pole in the middle. You can see through the walls in certain parts. It is a simple life with cattle as the main industry.*

*I am carrying a sense of melancholy and disappointment after just being rejected by my father-in-law. He is one of the elders of the village and has significant influence. I see him sitting beside the chief of our people. For years, I have been trying to get the respect of these men, wanting to make my contribution to the village. I came to him with a plan to move our cattle to other places for feeding. In front of everyone, he told me I was a fool, that I didn't know what I was doing. Now I feel shut out.*

*He has always been contemptuous of me. He never accepted me. He only let me marry his daughter because it was what she wanted. She is his favorite.*

*I am very angry, and I am going to hurt him by hurting my wife. I push her, verbally abuse her, and treat her as if she is nothing. There is a hardness in me now. I take her sexually whenever I want, ignoring her feelings.*

*Contributing to the village is important, especially for a man. Not being able to do this emasculates me. I need to feel powerful in some way. My wife has borne me no children and that is another reason why I feel diminished and annoyed with her.*

We go to another scene in this life.

*My father-in-law has just humiliated me once again in front of the other men. He rejected my ideas and dismissed me, saying, "You are a vicious fool!"*

*Now I am inside our hut standing over my wife's body. I just sexually assaulted her before beating her to death.*

*I run. The village is on a rise, and I am running down the hill toward a forest. I can hear the people in the village stirring as they realize what has happened.*

*The others are coming after me, and I feel panicked. I trip and fall. Because of my terror, I'm not thinking clearly. I stumble and fall again, near a stream. The ground is slippery, and before I get up, they are upon me. I am beaten and dragged back to the village. They spread my arms and tie them to a horizontal log. Then they throw me into a fire. I feel relief that it is all over.*

*I am floating above the village where I see my father-in-law weeping. I am pleased that I have finally hurt him so deeply that he is in tears. Now I am in darkness, floating in space with my shoulders slowly rotating around in circles, moving into a tunnel. I am feeling quite sick. Suddenly I am back in the village, looking down on my father-in-law who is saying something to my cooking body. I am trying to hear.*

*He is screaming at me, "I curse you to an eternity of life as a worm. You are scum. You will never be a man. I will follow you through eternity." He is repeating this over and over while kicking at the bones and flesh remaining on the fire.*

*I am floating up again. There seems to be a presence on my righthand side taking me by the arm and guiding me off to the right.*

*We are sitting in the same field where I have been before, an undulating slope like rounded-off terraces. It is Gabrielle, my guide. We sit on the grass, and she is saying, "These are the consequences of your actions."*

I ask Terry what she means by "consequences."

*She is telling me that this life was a turning point, the beginning of being caught in a loop, a loop that feeds itself. The way my father-in-law treated me, the burning and the curse, is what I created. My attitudes and actions feed this loop.*

*My head is in my hands, and I am sobbing. I haven't been told this before, and I am in shock. I wasn't aware of what I was doing.*

*The decision to seek retribution from my father-in-law by assaulting and killing his daughter leads to a cascade of negativity, building the loop. When I was first created as a soul, this path as a perpetrator was an option. The decision to take that path is a choice, an exercise of free will as a human. Gabrielle, the guide, says it isn't a wrong decision. There are no wrong decisions. Experiencing pain is important because it sinks you deeply into the human experience.*

*I feel shame at the way I was treated, and then I feel shame at the way I treated my wife. The father-in-law's curse vibrates through my soul and intensifies the shame. As my lives progress, I build the loop with my anger and bitterness. I act out my anger, and I reap the awful consequences. The loop grows strong and robust.*

From the beginning of his incarnations, Terry's soul had agreed to be tested. In this pivotal life, his father-in-law baited him. He had several choices—to remain a victim, to respond by standing up to his father-in-law, or to seek revenge. Killing his wife was a vengeful act that took him down a treacherous path. Instead of protecting his wife, like he did in previous lives, his hate and anger took over. This was an act of free will, and free will is sacrosanct in this system. Because we reap the consequences of our decisions, it is how we grow.

## Carrying the Curse

Terry says that after his father-in-law curses him, he feels his only power is to destroy others. I ask if he knows how curses are carried into subsequent lives.

*Words are vibrations. Vibrations are codes that can travel with you through your lives. The codes enter the DNA and the DNA travels with you as code through your lives. Because I was in a vulnerable state, just after dying in the fire, the vibration of those words penetrated my soul.*

Following that curse, Terry was caught in the loop. The "loop" is really the hundreds of years he spent in his dark night of the soul. He lives many violent lives before a turning-point life in the thirteenth century. He has built such a robust wall around him with so little empathy that he fights brutally in many wars and other violent situations. He sexually assaults and tortures people. And he is sexually assaulted and tortured himself. He is so shut down he feels very little—emotionally or physically.

> *I'm immune to the inhumanity of torturing people. I have their lives in my hands, and I whimsically choose whether they die slowly or quickly. This gives me a sense of power, but this is the only power I have. In other areas, I don't feel powerful at all.*

After twelve hundred earth years of experiencing this devastating path, Terry's soul is ready to start a turnaround. The elders carefully plan a life that is designed to begin his reformation. A closely connected soulmate agrees to play a crucial role.

## Beginning the Turnaround

In this life, Terry is a Christian soldier named Peter. Peter takes part in the notorious Fourth Crusade that sacked Constantinople in 1204. Our guides give us only what we can cope with, so, in an earlier regression when we visited this past life, Terry did not see the full desecration that the crusaders inflicted on the women and children of that city. Now, Terry is stronger and ready to see the truth. Terry describes his actions as Peter.

> *The streets are quite steep and cobbled. Evening is coming, and people have pots over fires. I smell smoke. We charge in on our horses, screaming and waving our swords around, chopping at the women. They run, and we chase them. I see dead women lying in the streets with their bellies cut open.*
>
> *I am separated from the others now. I dismount from my horse and walk casually from door to door, still killing. I stride right up and face people before I cut them up. I am kicking open timber doors, going into courtyards, killing women and children, anyone who is there. I feel noth-*

*ing. I just chop them up, look at their mutilated bodies on the ground, and walk away.*

*I am going next door. A group of people are cowering, backing away and screaming. I slice them up before walking out and going to the next house. The whole army is doing the same thing, all throughout the city.*

*I am sexually assaulting someone now. I cut her throat. Something about what I have just done has shaken me. Suddenly I walk out, feeling different. I have shocked myself out of the madness. My sword is in my hand, hanging by my side. Now I am looking at a number of terrified people waiting to be slaughtered, but I walk straight past them and out the door, shutting it as I leave.*

*Back on my horse, I am trotting up a hill in the opposite direction from whence I came. I am curious about what just happened, wondering how I managed to abuse and kill so many people. I feel like I have been in a trance and I just woke up. I am thinking how we were supposed to bring God to the unsaved, to the infidels, but instead we were encouraged to kill. Killing became normal until I woke up.*

After the crusade, Peter goes back to England to confront the monk who sent him to this holy war. He is bitter, full of anger, blaming the monk for sending him to slaughter innocent civilians. The frightened monk kills him in the church by stabbing him with a knife.

Terry is given an important insight. The woman he sexually assaulted and murdered in Constantinople is his soulmate, his beloved current wife. He realizes she sacrificed herself to break the loop. This moves him deeply. We sit silently for several minutes.

After this turning-point life, Terry's soul continues his journey back to connection. He has much to learn.

# The Struggle Back

After the turnaround, Terry still struggles with his violent impulses. In one life, he sees himself on the deck of a square rigger with others laughingly shooting the innocent inhabitants of an island.

In another life, he is an ordinary member of a community in love with the chief's daughter. He is a young, simple man but good at fishing. He is afraid but encouraged by others to ask the chief for her hand. Unfortunately, her father has other plans for her. The young man is killed for his audacity and clumsiness.

> *Now I am floating away above the treetops. On either side of me, two beings guide me away from the earth. I am sitting in the park with them. They are talking to me. They say, "You need more practice at speaking your mind." I understand they mean expressing my point of view, the art of negotiation. That life was about the start of learning how to do that.*

Terry's soul has many lives where he is loved, where he suffers loss, and where physical sensations and emotions gradually return.

> *All the dark stuff sticks to you like tar as you go through your lives. When it dries, it cracks off. Some of it falls off of its own accord and some you have to pick off. When you become aware, light comes through the cracks and it becomes easier to let it go, like picking cracked toffee off a toffee apple. When you heal, it leaves a residue on you. You are guided to do what is needed. There is no point worrying about what you are carrying until you are aware that it is there. Your attention will be drawn to it when the timing is right.*

In his immediate past life, Terry fought in the First World War.

> *I see trenches, smell gun smoke, and hear gunshots. My ears are buzzing. I am a young bloke, and there are dead people all around me in a trench. I don't want to be here.*

He survives the war and vows to never kill again. Residing in a little stone cottage overlooking a village in Scotland, he never marries and lives a solitary life. He is afraid. He knows he can kill without feeling, but he doesn't want to. He spends much of his time sitting up high above the village, looking down at green hills, watching the colors of the dawn and sunset while living a life of quiet and calm. But in that life, he avoids connecting to anyone. He doesn't know how to interact with people. He is so used to war.

Until he did the regressions, Terry was still carrying some of the remnants left over from all these challenging past lives.

*I am getting an image of sweeping the crumbs off a table after the feast is eaten. The crumbs are the journey I have taken through the regressions, and the feast is the many lives I lived. The feast is satisfying. I have learned much and now I better understand human nature.*

As part of "brushing the crumbs off the table," I ask Terry to renounce the original curse of his father-in-law that propelled him deeper into his perpetrator lives. I ask him to speak with conviction the following words:

*I reject that I am not a man and cannot be a man. I am a man in every positive sense of that word. I am a man with an open heart.*

## Reconnecting

Before he completed the regressions, Terry was afraid of being close to his wife and others, and deeply bothered by his thoughts of sexual predation.

*Because of my fear of acting violently, I locked myself away. My wife was rattling my doorknob to get in, and that felt threatening to me. I wanted to open that door, but I was afraid. I never wanted to hurt anyone again, and I didn't trust myself.*

*I have had lifetimes of using sex as power. I am completely releasing that now. There is nothing without the beauty of connection. I am seeing a lotus flower, sacred and beautiful, representing authentic sexual connection.*

He also had many headaches, finally discovering their source.

*The many headaches I get, especially on the left side of my forehead above the eye and at the base of my skull, come from my resistance. Being locked down takes constant energy. Keeping the door shut on my feelings is exhausting.*

Terry spent his life working hard to meet his obligations to his family, but he felt the heaviness of this load. He is given insight into this burden.

*The guilt I feel in taking time for myself comes from my feelings of obligation, my sense of needing to make amends. Now I know I have no reason to feel guilty. I do have obligations but, in the past, I fulfilled them from a sense of guilt, which always felt heavy. Now I will fulfill them lightly, "wanting to" rather than "having to," joyfully doing what needs to be done.*

We ask Terry's guide, Gabrielle, about the heavy path Terry's soul has taken during his earth journey. She gives us important information.

*The majority of souls do take a dark path. It is about gaining balance. One of the purposes of coming to earth is to experience the dark. Earth was built for it. Other places are lighter, softer, and gentler than earth, and not as good for learning.*

We discover that the father-in-law who cursed him in that past life, two thousand years ago, shares the same soul as Terry's current father. This explains an unusual incident that happened after Terry's first regression.

Two days after that first session, Terry had a serious accident at work that severed a part of a finger. The physical nature of his occupation meant Terry could not work for several months, so he was given time off with full pay. During this period, his father was dying. Terry's father had been a difficult man, so their relationship was not easy. His father expressed much torment as his life drew to a close. Nevertheless, Terry loved his father and spent two months taking him to his medical appointments, sitting with him, talking to him, and being at his side when he died. Terry's "accident" was no accident at all.

Terry wrote me an email after his father passed.

*Without the guidance you and two others gave me to open my heart and drop old baggage no longer of any use to me, I wouldn't have been available to my dad.*

*I would not have been calm enough, still enough, or patient enough to stand quietly beside my father as he embraced his mortality. I would not have been able to sit beside him on his last day and just hold his hand. I would not have been able to cradle his head in my hands, gently stroking his face and reassuring him that everything was okay when he woke two hours before he died, with horror and fear contorting his features. Thank you for the part you played that allowed me the honor to attend to my father.*

In his final regression, Terry successfully faced his last demons: his sexual thoughts and compulsions. Gabrielle told Terry that he has completed over ninety percent of his earthly lives. He is on the downward run of his soul journey, and his future lives will be a consolidation of all that he has learned. He will be given the opportunity to love and guide others who will benefit from the experience, compassion, and wisdom he has developed.

A few weeks after his last draining regression, which included the complete story of the crusader, Terry sent me an email.

> *It has taken me a while to bounce back from our last session. The next day, Saturday, I was crying on and off all day and felt flat and tired for the next two weeks. This last week I have felt free. That is the word that I keep using when I check in on myself. Free. My mood has lifted, and I am no longer feeling driven as I was prior to our session. Thank you once again for providing all I needed to face this part of myself.*

At last contact, Terry had just finished his first year studying kinesiology, planning to complete the diploma in the following year. He reported continuing his personal growth, founded in the work he and I did together.

I know it took a lot of courage for Terry to face the inner demons of his past, to bring them into the light where they were dissolved with unconditional love and understanding. He completed many lifetimes of confronting experiences before undertaking some lives that included opportunities for quiet contemplation.

## Conclusion

We have lifetimes to experience and then lifetimes to reflect and grow our understanding of ourselves and our journey. Because we tend to live longer lives in our current era, we have the opportunity to experience challenges in our life and, as well, reflect and integrate what we have learned. The current lives of many people in this book were designed to create opportunities for contemplation. That is why they undertook their regressions: to figure out the nature of the challenges they have faced and why. Many reading this book will be on the same journey, curious about their lives and keen to clear any blocks to fulfilling their life purpose.

One of the first steps is vicariously exploring the journey of others. To that end, we now look at those acting out their deep inadequacies by dominating others. They appear arrogant and entitled, with no care for their victims and no inkling of how destructive they are. Why do they oppress and misuse others? Are they trying to prove how powerful they are?

In the following chapters, we explore the need for domination more deeply.

# CHAPTER 5
# THE DARK PATH OF VAMPIRISM AND DOMINATION

In our scientific, modern world, vampires are fantasy creatures. They are portrayed as humanlike beings who feed off the blood of their victims. In other cultures, especially in the past, people believed vampires to be real—creatures or entities who steal energy from others.

The main quality of vampires, evident in all cultures, is their parasitic nature. They prey on the good nature of others to fill their emptiness, weakening their victims' life force, which gradually ebbs away.

Vampires don't just exist on earth. Cosmic black holes are also like vampires. A black hole is a tight, dense mass that sucks in light and energy from anything that comes too close. Its gravitational pull is so intense that anything captured cannot escape, including light.

## Energy Vampires

These days, we use the term "energy vampires" when referring to those people who consistently drain us. Such people take up a lot of the interactive space. Typically, they talk incessantly (usually about themselves), often overreact, and are not always truthful. While having little capacity to emotionally support others, they are attention-seeking and emotionally needy.

Some years ago, I read an article online about micro black holes.[7] The article put forward the possibility of small black holes existing all over our solar system. I immediately thought, "I know some of those."

Most probably, you do too. Dealing with these energy-hungry souls is not easy, but it explains why we have the concept of vampires in so many cultures. By maintaining healthy boundaries, we can prevent these empty people from leeching our energy.

Energy vampires can kill suddenly or slowly. Some years ago, I remember a woman coming to see me about problems with her son. He lived in her house with her two grandchildren and a couple of other people. The son was verbally abusive and sometimes violent. My client feared for the welfare of her grandchildren. As well as this concern, she was already ill, and her health was deteriorating.

This man was easily capable of physically hurting the children during his rages. He was already doing much psychological damage. By not acting, his mother was carrying *his* karmic burden.

I explained that the solution involved setting boundaries and making him face the consequences of his actions. She could ask him to leave, and if he didn't, the next time he became abusive, she should call the police. She objected, saying she couldn't do that to a family member.

I have met many individuals who stay in these types of relationships. The energy vampire usually complains, criticizes, dominates, or demeans. Victims think they are being caring by putting up with this behavior when in fact they are being weakened, sometimes to a point where they no longer have the energy to leave.

---

7. Charles Keeton and Arlie Petters, "Tiny Black Holes" NOVA, October 30, 2006, https://www.pbs.org/wgbh/nova/article/tiny-black-holes/.

In the regressions, I've seen many clients whose vital force has been stolen in their current and past lives. After the "vampire" has worn them out, these people are usually discarded and left wondering why these perpetrators have behaved in such selfish and callous ways.

Some souls choose the extreme path of separation. These souls are not only disconnected from Source and others, they have disconnected from themselves. They are extreme representations of vampirish behavior because they are empty; their survival depends on their ability to live off the energy they absorb from dominating others. But how does that work?

In this chapter, we explore two cases where the vampiric behavior is extreme. The first demonstrates vampiric transfer of energy and the way it becomes an addictive cycle, while the second explores the path out of domination.

## Vampiric Behavior and Its Consequences

In the first case, Rachel regressed into a past life as a young man. This man had been conscripted to fight in a war, which deeply damaged him emotionally. This life proved to be the grimmest of all the past lives we accessed during Rachel's regressions, as her soul became deeply lost and cut off from Source. She described it as "trudging into muddy, swampy places where you develop strong legs." The young man needed strong legs as he struggled through life alone without any help from a higher power.

We access the past life just after a brutal battle has taken place. The soldier is feeling strong emotions.

*I feel a ball of rage inside and a lot of shame about what we did in the battle. I see a very big wall and camps outside. We were ordered to kill everyone indiscriminately: men, women, and children. I am young. I hadn't killed anyone before and, while I did what I was told,*

95

*I cannot see a good reason for doing it. I see that they are people, just like we are. I look at their faces full of fear and confusion, so helpless, and yet we kill them.*

*I am getting glimpses of fighting soldiers, and that's what I expected, not killing helpless women and children. Afterward, our leaders explain that these people are not like us and they have to die for the greater good. We are told to channel our doubts into rage while fighting the soldiers, as they are the ones who left their own people unprotected.*

*I turn my initial shame and confusion into fighting, and I can't turn it off. I don't know how to stop. The wall inside of me is so big and so strong.*

To cope, the soldier buries his shame, cutting off any emotional vulnerability and feelings of empathy. Rachel describes him as feeling numb. He has no compassion for those he slaughters. When the war is over, he becomes a mercenary and leader of a loyal band of former soldiers.

*I see a battlefield. I get flashes of cutting people with a sword, especially across the neck and stomach, seeing blood, mud and dirt, hearing muffled sounds getting louder, now metal on metal, chinks and scrapes, men yelling and screaming—all of this noise zooming in and out because I am concentrating on what I am doing. I am killing people.*

*We outmatch the people we are fighting, so it's a slaughter. I think we are English, wearing chainmail, former faithful soldiers and now battle-hardened mercenaries. The opposition is not like us. They are locals wearing blue tunics and some odd bits of chainmail.*

*We are taking over this village. I can hear a bell ringing. It feels like we are doing it for a noble, but it is my thing. I am the leader of this group. We are killing and sexually assaulting and generally creating chaos. We kill all able-bodied men and many others, including women and children. We are brutal, putting no value on these people's lives whatsoever.*

*In the back of my mind there is something about it not being right, but I ignore it. I am cold, hardened by battle, and not wanting to feel anything.*

*There is something satisfying about pushing my sword into warm, soft flesh and ending a life. I find a certain peace that comes with the sword going in and the blood coming out. I cannot trust the world around me, but the kill is real. My body is hard with lots of scars. I have survived because I turn the hits I should've taken onto someone else. There is a righteousness in killing, which is proof of my power every time I kill. I am stronger and, if I wasn't, I would be killed.*

*In killing women, I kill my own vulnerability and sensitivity. I am railing against any frailty or feeling, purposely shutting myself down. When I kill, I cut off all the softness and keep getting harder, stronger, and leaner. I am used to wearing armor, and I am trying to create an internal armor.*

Killing, when one is this emotionally empty and isolated, creates a blood lust in the murderer. The mercenary comes out of time and space, experiencing a cathartic discharge when he sees the bloodletting. At the same time, he receives an energy charge from defeating his opponent. Now he becomes a vampire. The victim's life force is released, and the murderer absorbs this energy like a hit of adrenaline. He needs this energy because he has cut himself off from Source. Like any artificial high, it doesn't last. He is caught in a cycle of seeking more energy hits.

Rachel is disturbed by the intensity of her feelings as the mercenary. This reminds her that when she was young, she was mean and a bit of a bully. She pauses to reflect on her feelings.

*I have always been violent in my mind. I hate the idea that I would hurt someone badly because I am still carrying that angry energy from the mercenary. I don't like being a "hot" person; I want to be cool, calm, and peaceful, like a placid lake rather than a volcano.*

After acknowledging Rachel's discomfort with what she is receiving, I suggest we find out what happens to the mercenary. She reconnects with him in the past life.

*We take the village. Having fealty to the noble, I am rewarded with the keep, but I can feel a resentment growing toward him.*

*He didn't come and fight these battles. He didn't even go to war. He expects loyalty but he hasn't earned it, not in the way I have with my men. I have no fear of my men turning on me. They respect me as their leader. I am plotting to kill him in order to be the overlord. I am stronger than him so, in my view, overtaking him is fair.*

*After fighting my way into his castle, I slit his throat. I see the confusion on his face. He didn't realize what he unleashed in me. I am not going to sit quietly because there is never enough power for someone like me. Now I have to kill anyone of significance, including his family and hangers-on.*

*I can see a woman being kept alive, his sister or his wife, and I am going to make her mine. I am not going to love her. She is nothing more than my property. But I feel this thing inside, a vulnerability that is trying to push through. I have to drown it out, and I do that with violence. I sexually assault her to keep my vulnerability away. I hit her, throwing her around and attempting to suffocate her.*

*When there is no war, I have to do worse things. In peacetime, there is a silence, and the inner voices and vulnerability surface. I have to act to keep them away.*

Reliving this brutal violence distresses Rachel. I encourage her to breathe deeply. As soon as she calms down, she receives more information.

*I also have this pattern in my current life. When the vulnerabilities and softness come in, I put on my headphones to drown out the voices. I drink to numb my feelings. I even have vertigo to distract me. Being ill can be an escape too. I had one friend who would get sick; she was deaf to everything.*

*To face who you are, you have to hear these voices. "Are you doing the right thing? Are you being honest with yourself and others? Are your actions in alignment with your true self?" These are the voices that call your attention to your behavior, voices calling you to face a world that is not easy to see and hear. You run from what you see as difficult or negative.*

*You need to know that your lessons don't go away. They just get more insistent. People have mental breakdowns, illnesses, accidents, marriage break ups, job losses, and so forth, all to wake them up.*

After Rachel has shared this wisdom, I suggest we go back to the story.

*The woman I treat so cruelly slits her wrists, killing herself. I go into a rage, smashing things. I am furious that she has taken away my control. The voices are louder now, and I have lost the thing that drowned them out.*

*I am locking people out of the room, and I think of killing myself. Instead, I go back to war and fight, dying on the battlefield. I am glad to go, but I am not content with the way I lived my life. It was a hollow life, the worst kind of life, a life full of disregard for everyone with no connection to anyone.*

*I am looking around at the destruction, feeling confused. My spirit has been ignored all my life, and now suddenly it is let out. I am not physical anymore, and my physical self was everything. It is like meeting yourself for the first time, like a newborn lamb stumbling around.*

In fact, this mercenary's spirit has been stuck in a confused state for hundreds of years. Rachel now has the opportunity to release this stuck energy.

*I am like a child spirit. I want someone to come for me. They both come now, my guide and my eternal mother. They left me there for a time to take in what has happened. They are very understanding. We float away into the white light. Still confused, I ask them what happened.*

*It seems I couldn't get through to my real self. It was a challenging body and mind to be in. I was so strong-willed. Killing the pagans and being manipulated by the leaders to create rage shut me down and put me on that path of being hard and murderous. If I hadn't hardened, I wouldn't have survived.*

*That hardness, to some degree, was there in my subsequent lives, but those bodies didn't promote it like [the body of] the vicious fighter.*

*The shutting-down is most prominent in my current life. Sometimes I feel violent, and I want to smash things. When I tap into that rage, there is nothing else. Meditation and silence can be hard for me because the rage surfaces. The rage is a feeling but without a target. I am very connected to my inner warrior self. I experienced shame in my childhood being in a family that is against emotions and vulnerability. All that has encouraged me to shut down again.*

Rachel realizes her current life was planned to deliberately surface memories of this past life. Her body was carefully chosen, as were the challenges she has faced.

*What is important right now is my awareness of this shutting down, what caused it, and how it is being resolved. Only recently we've had the tools to access our past lives easily and receive help. One wouldn't want to re-live that past life alone.*

*The guides are telling me there was a lot of useful experience in that past life. I was learning to understand what healthy male energy is by experiencing its opposite. The mercenary's actions did not reflect authentic masculinity.*

The mercenary was stuck in violence because he'd cut himself off from Source. He was empty, unable to receive any loving attention. He perversely lived on the energy he reaped by killing others. But he died disillusioned. What he did to the nobleman's wife had an impact on him. In the beginning, he was disconnected from the pain he was causing her. But when she killed herself, he was affected. He was angry because he felt out of control. She took his power away, and he started realizing what he had done. Rachel reflects on the importance of listening to guidance.

*We don't listen because we are scared. We get a message to do something that seems outrageous, like go to Alaska and be an artist. It is our fear and our focus on survival that object. We are afraid to trust our guidance. But not doing it means we have a life half-lived.*

*Being shut down in that life of brutality was useful because I didn't hear my inner voice. The main learning for my current life is to listen to my inner guidance.*

Lifetimes where we are cut off from our guidance and refuse to listen are still useful. We are stubborn, stumbling along alone, making a mess of our lives. Eventually, after sufficient isolation and suffering, we learn to value wise guidance and listen to it. Then we have the choice to act on it or not, which is an exercise of our free choice.

I ask Rachel to check with her guides about the rage she has harbored. Will it keep coming up?

*The body can surface feelings just from habit. Knowing what is happening will help. I need to be accepting when any angry feelings surface, remembering the pattern, breathing through the emotion, and allowing it to pass. As I retrain myself, my anger will dissipate.*

As well as carrying anger in her current life, Rachel regrets causing pain to others. She is aware of the lessons now, and it is up to her to integrate this new understanding by consciously choosing her reactions.

During a regression six months later, Rachel receives more information about the value of the mercenary's life.

*That life was part of me, and no life is wasted. I need to accept everything that got me to where I am right now and then look back with gratitude. The energies are all balanced by the time we ascend. There is no need for shame. It was one of the possible choices. We all learnt from that life.*

Since regressing to the mercenary's life, Rachel has also noticed significant changes in herself.

*I am more compassionate since I have remembered the mercenary's life. A lot of my anger is gone—it was like it was locked in a box with a dark heat and a slow, deep burn.*

*My guides are sending love and light to me now, reminding me that they love me and are always with me and that I am on the right path. When I die this current life, I will be going home, back to them. As you get closer to the end of the soul journey, it naturally gets easier.*

Mythological vampires came out at night to suck the life force of others. The mercenary's life shows how this myth might have been formed. Cut off from Source and inner guidance, very little, if any, light or wisdom penetrated his psychological armor, creating an inner vacuum that propelled his vampiric actions, ushering in his dark night of the soul.

The addictive behavior of these souls—ranging from the emotional manipulation of others all the way through to murder—briefly satisfies their emptiness, but no matter how much attention they receive, it is never enough. They are stuck in a cycle of self-loathing because of their awful behavior and their fear of vulnerable feelings.

People who behave so atrociously are numb inside and numb to the feelings of others. Perhaps you have noticed how painful it is to thaw exposed fingers that feel frozen on a really cold day. It hurts! When Rachel reflected on how lost and cruel she had been in a past life, she discovered that thawing a frozen heart or soul is many times more painful. Although this case gives us the opportunity to understand gruesome behavior, it does not excuse it. Perpetrators appropriately suffer the consequences of their actions.

## The Value of Devastating Lives

The experience of abusing our power can be useful, whether that is emotional abuse or physical. On this planet, we learn through experience. What we perpetrate on others we will later experience ourselves so we can understand both sides of violence. This gives us a deeper understanding of ourselves and others. As we grow in awareness, we learn to value life as precious and develop compassion for all beings. We learn discernment, knowing what particular actions will lead us down the wrong path. Eventually, we are able to consciously choose what we want to experience and what we do not.

In our next case, we see how a soul is developing this discernment.

Jun is a naturopath who comes to see me wanting to develop her spiritual path. She is curious about finding the balance between accepting and loving others while still protecting herself.

In the regression, she learns she has endured a series of lives in which she was submissive and victimized. It began with a life as a deformed girl who, abandoned by her family, starved to death, imprinting her soul with deep feelings of worthlessness. Jun's soul goes on to experience many more sad lives.

To break this cycle, Jun's soul incarnates as a man who acts out his feelings of insignificance by secretly and sadistically dominating others. He feels contempt for his victims who he sees as weak, but deep down he feels contempt for himself. By dominating others, he externalizes what he wants to kill off in himself: his own weakness and insignificance. In this past life, the man is found guilty of murder and spends many years in prison.

When Jun wonders why her soul went down this path of worthlessness, culminating in a life of dominating and murdering helpless people, she suddenly finds herself in an expansive room that is completely white. She holds a scepter with a crystal ball in her right hand and a fan of dark purple flowers in her left.

*I am in a calm place. It doesn't seem like earth. The scepter represents the male energies of strength and power while the fan creates a flow of a gentle breeze, representing the female energy of softness. Both are needed. Now I feel a presence in the room.*

*That merciless life was about learning to appreciate what I had. I needed to feel in control, but there is no need to try and control. You can just be.*

*I am struggling to accept my actions in that life. I need to forgive myself. In order to love myself, I need to love that man. We all have a bit of everyone in all of us, good and bad, dark and light.*

*I am being told [the life of domination] was a useful life. I was learning about compassion and how precious life is. I had a lot of remorse in jail and a lot of realizations. There are two sides to the coin, and we need to see both. It is like a measuring stick or set of scales so you can decide what you want.*

When I wonder why she had the life as the deformed girl who was abandoned and felt worthless, Jun is taken to the body selection area in her life between lives. Here, she chose a body for that life. From several potential bodies, she selected a frail little female body.

*I could have had a slightly easier life, but I wanted to challenge myself. I didn't realize how hard it would be. I am a stubborn soul. I wanted to do it this way. The life was important, planned to show me how to love unconditionally. In that life, I experienced the opposite. I experienced a lack of love. That is useful.*

While Jun is in the body selection area, I wonder what happened after her lives of victimization and domination and ask about the plan for the subsequent life.

*I am still stuck with worthlessness. It took a long time to process those lives. In the afterlife, I list all the things I did, using categories of positive and negative. I am now with a young male, a friendly guide, planning my next life. Together, we are mapping out some ideas. I am really afraid of making the same mistakes, so I am hesitant about coming back. He says I need to jump in and move on.*

## Planning Nurturing Lives

The fact that Jun's soul is involved in planning the subsequent life means the soul returned to the higher frequencies of the afterlife. The many remorseful years in prison increased the vibrational frequency of Jun's soul.

*The life we decide on is significantly different to the other lives. With help, we carefully choose a caring environment and a loving family in Japan.*

*I am to be a little boy, an only child to older parents. I'll marry and have one or maybe two children. I will be in a position of power, a lawyer in the government where I'll be secure. I will die of a heart attack at age fifty in 1952.*

We review that life to see if Jun's fears were realized.

*It went pretty well. I lived a simple life with a loving wife and good, respectful children. I felt love for them all. It was a loving environment. Work was hard but good. I felt valued there and worthwhile. I see the guide is holding two thumbs up.*

I ask if we can look at the plan for Jun's current life.

*It is a continuation of developing a sense of worthiness. It's import-ant to develop feminine energy in my current life. I was loving in that previous life, but I didn't always show emotion. I still don't outwardly show affection.*

*We are choosing a female body, Eurasian. I'll be well-off finan-cially, but I could get caught up in social issues, mainly the expectations of others. That is a challenge.*

*The plan is having a more balanced life, not focusing on one thing like success, work, or obsessing about a partner. I choose a family that has those balanced values, and I will find it easy to express love and not get caught in proving myself. This life is more about just "being."*

*The family's values are most important. The type of body is irrel-evant. So, the choice is made on the family that fits that criterion of appropriate values.*

The family Jun chooses turns out to be perfect for the contin-uation of her soul development. Jun's mother in her current life is Margaret, a sweet, soft-spoken woman, who comes for a regres-sion. It is soon apparent why she was chosen to be Jun's mother. During the regression, Margaret receives information about her soul journey, explaining that she is a loving, open soul, emanating peace and love. She is a perfect mother for Jun in her current life.

Jun is still recovering from her sense of worthlessness and needs love and positive attention. In her regression, she is given more information about her current life plan.

*To fulfill the plan, I need to be more open. I wonder how I can be accepting and loving and still protect myself. I still have a fear of being unprotected.*

When I ask about this fear, Jun immediately gets an image of the deformed girl.

*One side of my face is deformed slightly in the beginning, but it gets worse over time.*

*Now I am looking at her and seeing the real beauty in her soul, the courage of taking this on to teach me so much, especially compassion.*

*There is a golden light coming down now, which is nurturing, loving, and protecting. I lock eyes with her, and then I hug her. [Long pause.] This dear girl is okay.*

This healing action of feeling love and compassion for the brave young girl released Jun from her fear of being unprotected.

The dominating life was a significant turning point for Jun's soul, showing how exercising her free will enhanced her soul's recovery. When this man was in prison, he didn't waste much time brooding and feeling sorry for himself. He spent the time reflecting, trying to understand why he took such a devastating path. Jun's soul then had an opportunity to continue learning in the afterlife—and took it. This is why her soul progressed so quickly over a few lifetimes—from brutal carnage to fostering love.

Jun came from another planet a long time ago and has had nearly two thousand earth lives. As a soul, she is a healer. The journey through her many incarnations has been about developing the skills and understanding needed to heal others.

Jun is still in the process of emerging from her challenging past lives. She has learned much and has more to learn, especially about being open and affectionate. As she develops, others will reap the benefits of her journey into the nether regions of the human experience.

## Conclusion

During the regressions I conduct, the guides consistently tell us that nothing is lost and much is gained by choosing the path of separation and isolation. They emphasize that each soul learns much by this choice. Nothing, according to the guides, is a mistake.

Of course, this view is challenging to us. We feel the anguish of loss and separation in both our bodies and our hearts. When our fellow humans treat us with indifference or cruelty, our disappointment runs deep. We are horrified at those who find satisfaction in hurting others, who revel in their misfortune, or who feed off their energy.

It is important to remember that all our actions have consequences. Rachel's soul took centuries to find its way back after taking a dark path. The same holds true for Yvette and Terry. While all three had lives as perpetrators, they also suffered many lives as victims.

The law of karma means our motivations matter just as much as our actions. Although facing the truth of our actions is sometimes deeply painful, it is essential if we wish to heal. We need to acknowledge the hurt we have caused others and feel compassion for those we have wronged—intentionally or not—and for ourselves, for we knew no better at the time.

Many of us carry deep feelings of worthlessness. Some of us blame our childhoods, our parents, or our partners for our struggles in life. For souls like Rachel, Jun, Yvette, and Terry, facing what they have done in their past lives and then forgiving themselves takes a lot of courage. Having lost ourselves in darkness, having inflicted our pain, hate, and anger on others, self-awareness is the key to restoring our connection.

In the next chapter, we further explore the transition of lost souls: how they begin to emerge into awareness after lives of transgression and violence.

# CHAPTER 6
# THE TRANSITION OF LOST SOULS

In the three previous chapters, we met souls who were cut off from Source. These souls spent many earth lives as perpetrators or victims. Yvette relished the suffering of the slaves she traded. Overcome with blood lust, Terry rampaged through Constantinople, abandoning himself to his worst instincts. Rachel, the vampiric mercenary, and Jun, the intimidator, energetically fed on the carnage they wrought upon others. All experienced both victimization and domination. During their lost lives, these souls chose to disconnect from higher vibrational levels, refusing any help from their guides.

These lives aren't easy. Powerful experiences can imprint on souls and manifest in subsequent lives. Souls choose to take this journey into isolation and separation. But it can be so devastating and confusing that some struggle to find their way out.

After death, some souls refuse to return home, but that really is a choice. There are reasons for this reluctance. Some are angry and willful, some feel unloved, some are confused, most have lost trust in Source. Whatever is the case, the soul has agreed at some level to go down this path.

Eventually, when souls realize they are stuck and isolated, other souls and guides will come to help. The lost souls are given a choice. They can move back to their spiritual home to study or undertake an incarnation—one that is carefully designed to help them grow. In this chapter, see how lost souls make their transition back toward the light.

## Souls Can Choose to Be Lost and Found

Souls can become lost unwittingly, or they may deliberately choose to take a dark turn. Sometimes, a soul's disconnection is purposely planned at a higher level. One client, Frances, discovers a soulmate of hers has been completely stuck. We explore how this happened.

Frances is from a soul group that set up a serious experiment. Another member of the group, Perdita, was to become lost, with Frances being chosen to rescue her. This experiment took place over hundreds of years and many lifetimes. Frances explains why they were undertaking the experiment.

> *It is like we were asking the question, "Is it possible to lose souls and is it possible to find them?" It does feel really risky. It feels like I am not the one who is making all the decisions. There is no fear though. It is something about finding out what it's like being disconnected. It is a collective curiosity about pushing the boundaries.*

Perdita had several difficult lives before incarnating as a young girl who was abducted. She was isolated in a cabin with a man twenty years older and forced to submit to his wishes. Because Frances and Perdita are connected at the soul level, Frances explains how Perdita became lost.

> *In her heart she was strong, but physically she was frozen, feeling small and powerless. She was afraid and confused but had nowhere to go. Eventually she felt so threatened, she left, walking out into a cold, snowy landscape. She kept looking back, afraid he would come after her once he discovered she was gone.*

*I see her now in a marketplace of people selling wares and chickens. She is pushing herself into the crowd of people, wishing that people would acknowledge her. She feels invisible. People don't see her. She is screaming, shouting for help, but no one is taking any notice.*

*Perdita didn't realize she was dead. She was so intertwined with the physical, so immersed in the amnesia, that she completely forgot who she really was. She was lost. I have an image of looking on Perdita's life, as if she is in a snow globe screaming for help.*

*I had several lives to develop the skills I needed to help her. The tools I have now were able to penetrate through to her. We [in the soul group] had to all stay calm while reaching her and releasing her. Until we found her, we had felt apprehensive.*

Frances connected energetically with Perdita to warm her up and help her realize that she was now found and safe.

Once Frances connected with Perdita, there was great joy in the soul group.

*Perdita joins the soul group. They are welcoming her and embracing her.* [Crying.] *It is a family bond energetically. I have such a sense of relief.* [Crying loudly and deeply.] *It feels like I have rescued a lost part of myself.*

*It was a mission, and I have a sense of pride from someone saying, "You have done a really good job." We [the soul group] had a feeling of not knowing where to look. There was much distress in Perdita in those final moments before she died, which locked her into that disturbing energy.*

*Now there is this huge feeling of relief, as if I had almost given up. It is coming to me that a soul can make a decision to surrender into the life and decide to disconnect.*

Souls are curious, and some souls are willing to take risks. Frances's soul group created an experiment to increase their knowledge. Fortunately, their experiment worked, and Perdita was recovered.

Perdita decided to be cut off and lost. Other souls, like Yvette in the slave trader case, chose to spend many centuries isolated. I wonder how these souls return from their isolation and begin reincarnating again.

## Lost Souls Can Choose to Return to Earth

As we have seen previously, souls can be lost in isolation for a long time, disillusioned with others and Source, and not wanting to reincarnate. But there comes a time when the monotony drives them to seek something more.

Sophia, who you met briefly in chapter 1, learns that she had a number of lives as perpetrators and victims. She has reconnected to her higher self and is on her way back to the light. When I ask what it is like being lost, she is told she is not to move in that direction anymore. It is too risky for her soul, but she can share how souls return to earth.

*These souls sit on their own for a very long time. They sit and sit. They want to be alone and don't want to come in contact with anyone. Eventually, they realize they are missing out, and that is how they end up back in another life. Underneath there is a selfish driver. They reincarnate, but not because they want to grow and develop.*

*No one puts them in the dark, they choose it and think and brood. They only come out of it for gain. They don't come out to give, but at least they've reached a point where they want to come out and are willing to incarnate to balance their karmic debt. But it is not done with love; it is done as a bargain, and we [their spiritual guides] hope they'll use their free will to learn and become better souls.*

I have met people who are in this category, including some in religious and spiritual organizations. Many are compelled to help others, believing they will be rewarded. But this is more about themselves than the people they propose to help. Good deeds are worthwhile, especially when the person's intentions are pure. But the intentions of these souls are muddied by personal agendas. Driven to make something of themselves, they often override the will and needs of those close to them.

## Good Deeds Can Be Selfishly Motivated

One client relived two lives that demonstrate how a need for recognition can play out.

Mitch, aged forty, wants to know if he is on the right career path. He is divorced with a young son and works as a sales representative. We go to his first past life.

*I am in a jungle, exploring. There are about five or six of us, all men wearing safari suits. I feel like I am very cocky, and my cockiness has got us into trouble. It is going to get us killed.*

*Someone told me not to go there before we set out. I said, "It'll be all right." We are missionaries bringing the word of God to these people. I want to save everybody.*

*We are being confronted by the locals who have spears and are unfriendly. Headhunters. We are captured. I am preaching to them in English as they are carrying us along, but they don't understand me. We end up in their village. I watch my compatriots have their throats cut, feeling absolutely terrified before they cut mine.*

The missionary is so disturbed, he doesn't realize he is dead. By asking gentle questions, I help him adjust to the truth.

*I am looking down at my dead body. I am in shock. Someone comes to lead me away. Now I am in a hospital with nurses looking after me. Eventually I am well enough to come out of the hospital.*

*The Council of Elders is waiting and quite amused that I put myself into that situation.[8] I am still feeling shocked at what happened. I failed to achieve what I set out to do. The Elders are asking me how I could have done things differently.*

*I should have listened to advice. I am upset that my team was killed because of the decisions I made. It was a strong lesson for me to learn, to not be cocky and think I know it all. I need to learn to be respectful of other people's advice and experience. I was overconfident, believing I knew what I was doing after just a few successes.*

When I ask what was important about exploring his overconfidence, he is taken to another past life.

*I see houses with steep roofs and streets with horses and carriages. It seems European, perhaps Germany. I am a man, a lawyer around forty, well-dressed in a smart suit, walking to work in the morning. I feel confident because I know I am good at the work I do. I feel in control.*

*There is a ring on my finger, so I am married, but we have no children. My wife cannot have children and she feels that loss deeply, but it doesn't bother me too much.*

We progress to another scene.

*I feel like it is nighttime, and I am old, sitting in a chair in my house. It is a very nice house. My wife has passed. She never got over being childless and was depressed a lot. I am sad because I focused too much on work. I feel very alone. I wasn't there for her as much as I wished. I thought success was about focusing on the job. Now I don't have the job or career, just a big, empty house. I am wondering, "What was the point of it all?" I was out of balance and I feel the*

---

8. The "Council of Elders" is a term Michael Newton used to describe wise groups of beings who guide souls.

*heaviness of deep regret. There are servants in the house, but I am really alone, sitting in a chair drinking liquor.*

*Now I am in bed, very weak.*

He passes, somewhat unaware. Again, I ask questions to gently help him accept his death. Soon after, he sees his wife.

*I am really emotional, telling her how sorry I am. She is comforting me. We really did love each other.*

*I got caught up in the physicality of life and focused on being a provider. I put my clients first, not able to say no to them. I felt like they needed my help, so I had to help them, believing other lawyers were not as good as I was. There is a bit of ego in this belief. I couldn't turn people away, thinking I was indispensable. I worked really long hours while my wife sat at home, waiting.*

Mitch exercised his free will by doing what was important to him while ignoring the needs of his wife. This stance eventually threw his life right out of kilter.

*Now I have passed; she is understanding, forgiving, and loving, being part of my soul group and leading me home. She is taking me to a house, offering me tea. I can feel the love between us. She is saying that the way it was is how it was meant to be. I was to understand what is important in life and know that, at the end of it all, what really matters is relationships.*

Mitch soon discovers he ignored his intuitive guidance, which often comes in the form of a nudge.

*I ask if I followed my guidance. She says no, I didn't. I had a choice. I was nudged but I didn't listen. There was a time when my wife was sick. Instead of looking after her, I went back to work. She asked me to stay, to be with her, but I said I couldn't. Other times she wanted to go on vacation, but I said I was too busy. Some of my work colleagues suggested I go home, telling me that they had the work under control, but I would not let go. There was a perfectionist streak in me that was a challenge to overcome. It fed into my need to control.*

In each of his past lives, Mitch was driven to make a big difference in the lives of others while ignoring the needs of those close to him. In the first as a missionary, he ignored the dangers and egotistically pressed on. In the second, he neglected his wife, basking instead in power, success, and the admiration of his clients.

In earlier chapters we learned that feeling worthless drives bad behavior. Here, underlying feelings of worthlessness drive a need for recognition. Mitch is on the way back to connection, but his ego's needs were in the driver's seat.

In comparing his past lives with his current life, Mitch realizes he is beginning to shift. He used to put work first, but he cannot do that now if he wants to see his young son.

*Maybe I have a difficult ex-wife to help keep me on track. I get frustrated with her sometimes because she wants to be in control, cutting the time I have with my son. I can't negotiate with her, so I have to make my son a high priority if I want to see him, and I do.*

Mitch is reaping what he has sown: an ex-wife who is as willful as he was. In the past life, he never gave ground to his wife and always did what he wanted. But he is adjusting, no longer needing to focus on outsiders to make himself important and bask in their admiration. His new mission is caring for those close to him.

When we are generous, how do we know whether we are being selfish or selfless?

The key lies in our expectations. Pure generosity wants nothing back, not even gratitude or recognition. We have no need to be paid back and little interest in the outcome of our altruism.

# Lost Souls Can Choose to Return Home

Lost souls don't really understand people. Unwilling to risk being hurt, they prefer to be alone. As we have seen, this desire for isolation continues after death. These souls stay lost until they choose to reform by cleaning themselves up. Most souls do eventually choose redemption. The next case demonstrates how a deeply separated soul returns to his soul home.

During several regressions, Ryan relived a number of perpetrator lives, learning his soul had been stuck in lower frequencies for hundreds of years. In these incarnations, Ryan's soul was like a vampire. He used the energy of people he manipulated to continue incarnating in perpetrator lives. In these lives, he died horribly. He was so numb he didn't feel anything, but his death always came with a twist. He enjoyed manipulating people's emotions. For example, he would spend a lifetime convincing everyone he was evil. Right at the end, when he was being tortured and executed, he'd prove he'd been innocent all along. Then he would watch their horror as he died. The self-doubt he created in people gave him an energetic hit.

Ryan was profoundly lost and cut off. His larger soul and soul group wanted to help him return. This was a mammoth enterprise. Some soul relatives incarnated and sabotaged his strategy of surviving off the energy of others. They refused to be fooled by his act. Now Ryan's soul didn't get the energetic hit. He began looking for other opportunities. His guides intervened, and he agreed to incarnate into a carefully planned life.

He is born into a Puritan community. Later, a highly evolved soulmate incarnates as his daughter. Despite himself, Ryan learns to love her. Then she is accused of being a witch. She is only seven, but there is nothing Ryan can do to save her. Despite her innocence, she is burned at the stake. As she is dying, she gives Ryan a look of pure love. He screams out in emotional pain. His shell has been penetrated. Ryan explains what then happened.

*He had come to care for this young girl and, after her death, he wanted to kill himself, but he didn't. He had to live in the pain for a while. His death wasn't violent, but the return was. It took a long time to integrate the learnings from the soul being lost for so long.*

The return of Ryan's soul to his soul home caused a disruption. He had intense experiences during centuries of separation from his larger self. Integrating all the learnings and energetic changes at the nonphysical level took time. The final aspects of integration took place during his current life. He did many sessions of counselling and regressions over several years, which helped this process. We learned that integration needs to take place at the physical level as well as the nonphysical.

During Ryan's last session, he is told he has reintegrated his lost parts now and can keep pursuing his interests. He is very creative and successful, a scientist who brings useful inventions to market, making a positive difference in people's lives.

When lost souls like Ryan's don't go home after physical death to integrate their learnings, they can grow more and more destructive. If they become too estranged, they will experience a lot of suffering, then collapse before finding their way home. Ryan gained a lot of learning from his experiences, but his lives were not pleasant.

Balancing our need for learning with our need for connection is a more comfortable experience, and most souls will endeavor to do that. Few souls become as lost as Ryan's did. In his last session, Ryan made an important point, "We need to remember there is a place to come back to. We have a soul home."

## Stubborn Souls Can Stay Stuck

Children who are described as willful insist on their own way. Willful souls are the same. They don't like listening to authority or taking advice from others. Sometime previously, these strong-willed souls experienced loss, betrayal, or both. Now they don't trust anyone. They can come across as selfish and arrogant, believing they are the only ones who know what is right. Without the benefit of higher-level guidance, they stumble into unexpected disasters. This is useful, because they learn what not to do. But some souls become stuck in stubborn behavior. It can take many lifetimes before they learn to surrender their willfulness and return home.

Bree has a strong will. In her current life, she left her home and family, moving between countries where she chooses to live alone. Bree admits she is not close to people. She came to her regression with a few questions. Having never learned to swim, she wonders why she is so terrified of water. Although she has not suffered any specific violence in her current life, she notices violence around her. For example, a couple of days after she moved into a new apartment, a woman was murdered next door. Also, some of her friends are in abusive relationships. During her session, she experiences three past lives that reveal her very strong will.

In the first, she is a woman living in a cabin in a forest in North America. Her husband is accidently killed in the forest while chopping wood. She didn't know it at the time, but she was pregnant. The life that follows is lonely.

*Life is tough because I am mostly alone with this baby. I feed travelers by growing vegetables and herbs, baking bread, and making meals. I am managing, but it is stressful having the responsibility of this baby.*

119

*She cries a lot and that makes me nervous. My happiness is a brown dog, my only true companion, who is now sitting by the fire.*

Bree's strong will and independence help her survive. When I suggest she move to another scene, she finds herself in a different life in an earlier era.

Bree is with her wealthy father who wants her to marry, while she seeks adventure.

*I am twenty and very stubborn. He has been a loving father and given me everything I wanted. Now I want to explore. I won't give in. I want to experience life before I get married. I am continually repeating to him what I want and why I want it. I threaten to travel with or without his support. He wants me to be safe and providing for me is the best way to achieve this.*

*I board a ship for the Caribbean. Travelling there takes a long time, but it is worth it. I love the beautiful island where I settle. The sea is that beautiful aqua blue you find around coral reefs. I feel happy and relaxed.*

*To me, the people are friendly and exotic with their brightly colored clothing. My clothes are different. I wear a long, elegant dress of pretty blue, and I live in an attractive, stylish house containing beautiful furnishings in the European style. My servants look after the property.*

*I lead a pleasant, luxurious life socializing in lovely houses, chatting and drinking from elegant teacups while listening to talented hands playing calypso music. We are all English.*

We move to another scene in the Caribbean when Bree is now thirty-two and still alone. She walks to the beach at sunset, dressed in her elegant clothes and delicate shoes.

*It is so beautiful in the evening; I have done this a few times even though one of the servants told me not to go out alone. I am still stubborn, having no fear and doing whatever I want.*

In the growing darkness, she hears voices. Expecting to know these people, she strolls toward them.

*They are all men wearing shabby clothes and looking at me strangely. I am confused and suddenly afraid. My heart is racing. The path is dangerous for me in my fancy shoes so I cannot run back. I am stuck.*

*They speak a different dialect. I notice now there is a boat in the water. I sense they are dangerous, a gang of thieves.*

These men approach her, grabbing her fine jewelry. She insists they give it back.

*The jewelry was a present from my parents. I refuse to let it go. Even though I know this place is remote and I am alone, I still focus on my jewelry. I am determined to stop them from taking it.*

Her persistence, clutching at her jewelry, angers these men. They become violent.

*I begin to think that maybe I am not going to get out of this. They hit me and kick me harder and harder. I am in pain, crying out, getting weaker and weaker because there are too many of them. I see blood after a machete hits my head.*

*They have broken me. I am lying on the ground, too weak to resist, feeling really cold.*

I ask if she is dead.

*I feel cold but peaceful. I can see my body. I am standing on that rocky path. The sky is still beautiful.*

I ask Bree if she has any thoughts or feelings looking at that body.

*I feel sad. [Crying.] I feel really sad but also a sense of pride because, in my life, I did what I wanted. I managed to entice my father to help me make it possible. I was very independent and happy during the years I lived there. I felt so alive in this beautiful, amazing place, even though it was where I died. I am pleased with this short and happy life. I did what I wanted.*

Before the regression, Bree said she has carried a great fear of water all through her life. When I ask her to imagine being in the water, she immediately experiences physical feelings.

*I have a heavy weight on my chest, and I cannot breathe. I feel like I am in choppy water, struggling to breath.*

*I see a small boat that is empty. I am trying to get back to this boat, but the waves are stopping me, and I see it drifting away. I am very scared, panicking, thinking I am going to die. But I am very stubborn, still trying to get to the boat even though it keeps being swept away. I am swallowing a lot of water, going under but then struggling to get back up for air. I am becoming weaker and weaker, going under for longer periods of time.*

She continues reporting on her struggle to get to the boat, and each time it drifts away. I ask her if it is possible that she could have died.

*I feel very relaxed now in the water, with my hair flowing all around me. It is very quiet down here compared with the storm above that is shattering the peace with its thunder and lightning. Now I am floating in this peaceful silence.*

*I was a nineteen-year-old girl. I wanted to go out to sit in the boat and look at the stars. I was told not to go out at night, but I am stubborn. No one tells me what to do. I went out, and the weather turned, and a storm came quickly. I couldn't stop the boat drifting away from the beach, so I got out, trying to swim back to shore, but I was being swept out to sea, further and further away. In my current life, as soon as I go in the water, I feel afraid of the tow.*

Bree begins comparing her past lives with her current life.

*I see some links between the lives. I am still very stubborn. Even though people travel these days, one is still expected to settle down and have children. I haven't. Now I live far from my family, who live in Europe, free from their expectations, their oppression, and their judgment.*

*I didn't want children in that life in the Caribbean, and I still don't want children. From the widow's past life, I can see why I resist having children. She didn't enjoy her child at all. I am afraid of getting close to people and losing the ones I love. I don't want loss, and I never want to be a single mother with a baby.*

*I have always been stubborn. In each life, I have closed down to some degree. I don't take the advice of others easily. I am one of the most stubborn people I know.*

Stubborn people insist on the freedom to choose their own path. Bree was willing to pay the ultimate price for this freedom in two of her past lives. Although she has been stubborn in her current life, she is not cut off from her intuitive guidance. We know this because she was guided to see me. During her session, she was able to release trapped energies from those two past lives. Reflecting on those experiences may help her surrender some of her willfulness and listen more thoughtfully to the guidance of those who care for her.

Some people believe that surrender means defeat. Suggesting they could ease up on themselves triggers feelings of fear and vulnerability—the very emotions they seek to avoid. This is why some souls endure many troubled lives before learning to soften their stance.

## The Fate of Damaged and Deeply Lost Souls

Ethne experiences a past life as a navigator for Bomber Command during WWII. After bombing Dresden, his Lancaster was shot down and all the crew perished. The navigator passed quickly, and Ethne's soul recovered in a "hospital."

*It is like a transitional state, more of a healing place. There are quite a lot of us here. We are pretty damaged, but some have been through much worse.*

Our souls can be damaged, just as humans can be damaged. After a traumatic life or death, the energy of the soul can be all messed up. Ethne wants to assist the healers in this hospital. She is allowed to do this in a limited way.

*When the energy of these damaged souls is scrambled, I am shown how to smooth it out. I do it by pouring love into it, like gently strok-ing them with love to untangle it.*

*Sometimes the healers consult one another on how to heal damaged souls. [In their incarnations] some souls have been tortured or have tor-tured others. Some have killed and hated doing it. Others have taken their own lives. These souls need to stay here, in hospital, for a long time.*

She also notes that some souls are so deeply damaged, they resist the healing.

*It is like a matrix in that place. The love is always there, bathing us, there for us to take it in. But some are so damaged they cannot take it in. They are angry and really screwed up. Some of the skilled healers can deal with it, but I cannot even read the really traumatized souls.*

Ethne learns that some of the damaged souls leave before they can be healed.

*Some have been terribly damaged. They heal as much as they can so they can go back to earth without too much damage. But some of them won't let the healers heal them. They don't want to be completely healed. Some are so freaked out, the healers discharge them early, but*

*only if that is what these damaged souls want. There is no forcing any-
one up here. We all go to this place, but then it is our choice to what
extent we are healed.*

Next, she discovers that some souls can be so damaged they
are disintegrated. This means the death of the soul identity. From
what we've been told by the guides, no one in the higher realms
ever wants this to happen.

*There is a one-on-one healing place, like an isolation room where
the healers do all sorts of healing modalities. The damaged souls are
showered with acceptance. They can have visitors. They can stay
alone. Sometimes they can go back and be remade as a soul.*

I ask Ethne for more details on what it means to be remade as
a soul.

*This means their energy is broken up and reassembled. They would
only choose it if they believe they can never get over what has happened
to them. It is like being absorbed by a fire and becoming part of the
whole again. Then they have to start all over from the beginning, like
a new soul. Not many choose it, but it is an option. They have to
give up all that they have achieved. It is a surrender and only happens
when a damaged soul cannot face going on. Some don't want to heal,
and they don't want to keep going. They cannot open up to the healing. It can take a long time to come to this point when they are asked
to choose.*

In other regressions, guides have mentioned that deeply lost
souls can be disintegrated, but I am still surprised when I come
across a client who knew of a soul being broken up.

Valencia was just such a client. When she was young, she married Brad and had two children. The marriage was not a happy one.

*I never really loved my first husband. We lived together for eigh-
teen months and he was supportive, but the day we married, he totally*

*changed. For example, when I was in hospital from serious complications after childbirth, he didn't come to the hospital for eleven days. When he did, he screamed at me for not coming home.*

The marriage didn't last, and at age thirty-nine, Brad was killed in a car accident.

*When he died, I woke up in great pain and it all correlated with his injuries. Sometime later, I went to two psychics to contact him. Both got absolutely nothing, saying it was like he never existed, adding that they had never experienced that before.*

I suggest we explore this, so we ask the guides where Brad has gone.

*They just said he is not contactable on the other side. He went to a place where you go back to being nothing. He became nonexistent. It was a choice made by him and a panel of masculine energies. They talked about this last life and the many lives he had prior. He wasn't progressing. Over previous lifetimes, he was prepared. It was an outcome he accepted.*

I asked if he was always stuck in the lower frequencies between his lives.

*He had experienced the higher realms several times, but he remained like a child, an early soul. He just didn't grow.*

I asked how something like this could happen, wondering what could create such a state.

*I see a high-level class on the other side. They are creating, and some can create better than others. I picture someone like Harry Potter in a class with others, all creating with their wands. The creator of his soul was not very talented. Even creating souls is a learning. It is a totally different place from where we are. They are encased in their own little bubble for a specific purpose.*

*Brad's soul had problems from the beginning. Seems like he was missing something. They are showing me a large tangle of knots. He gave up during the last life and nothing mattered anymore. He stopped trying and was content with this outcome. It doesn't happen a lot.*

*When they do break up the soul, the energy is reused, and all the learnings are retained in the system.*

We think of ourselves as humans, but that is only part of the story. In fact, we are souls expressing our inclinations through a human body. Our incarnations can imprint the soul, and the soul carries these imprinted influences into subsequent lives. Souls can be stuck in various frequencies for hundreds of earth years. In the worst-case scenario, souls can become so disillusioned and dejected that they agree to be dismantled.

We can easily become confused about who we really are. Some of us think our true self is our soul. But this is not completely accurate. We are more than our soul. Our larger self invests energy in the earth system, stepping down vibrations to resonate at the lower levels. Although no one, including our soulmates and our guides, wants to give up on a soul, we need to know we are more than our soul. Our true self cannot be eliminated. We are vibrational beings that are part of a much larger self.

## Helping Lost Spirits Transition

Some people die sad, alone, and disillusioned. They may have been disappointed with their lives. Perhaps they feared death, feared eternal judgment, or felt unloved. If they died violently or suddenly, the shock may have thrown them into a state of confusion, a kind of purgatory. These spirits may need our assistance. Here is a case that illustrates how some of us can help these spirits return to their soul home.

127

Kelly is a palliative care nurse who loves her work in a caring and flexible hospice. For a couple of weeks, she is sent to the palliative care ward of another hospital to help out. In this large clinical hospital, she is greatly affected by the staff's impersonal approach to the dying. Soon after returning to her hospice, she comes to see me.

*I felt overwhelmed with the despair of the patients at that place. The nurses were not connecting. It is based on a medical model. The atmosphere was so melancholy, and the patients were so sad. For me, the energy was overwhelming. I had to walk outside every now and then to cope. The second day, I detached.*

I try to take Kelly into a trance to resolve her issues. Nothing much happens. She seems blocked. I suggest she go with whatever emerges.

She tells me she hears the word *why*.

"Why what?" I ask.

*Why am I here on this earth, and why am I here in the dark?*

I ask her where she is.

*I am going back to that large hospital. I can hear something. It is weeping.*

I ask her who is weeping.

*The souls, the lost souls. I am feeling their sadness.*

Kelly starts crying softly.

After giving her time to release this sadness, I suggest she sends love and light to them, letting them know that there are many of us here who love and care for them and want them to be found. There is a long pause.

*It's okay. They have gone to the light.*

*I am being told by the guides that I am doing important work with the patients I look after. The guides are all clapping. [Kelly cries.] I am receiving so much love and appreciation from them. They are very happy with me.*

*I came back from that large hospital in a huge depression. I have been in a little hole, and only just yesterday, I started to come out.*

A few days later, Kelly emails me.

*When I left the session and got into my car, I had such a beautiful experience of joy. It lasted forty-eight hours.*

At the moment of death, these poor spirits were trapped in their sense of isolation and despair. Kelly released this energy of sadness so these spirits could go home.

Sensitive people can sometimes sense spirits around them, perhaps when resting or meditating. Many people have been taught to be afraid of spirits. Once they understand that these spirits cannot hurt them and are only lost, they are usually willing to help. The intervention is extremely simple.

With the loving intention of compassion, send love and light to the lost spirits. When you sense you have their attention, let them know there is somewhere for them to go. You don't need to speak; they can read your mind. Suggest they look around for someone who will help—and don't be surprised when they suddenly disappear. That means they are on their way back to connection.

# Conclusion

Transitioning can be challenging for some souls and spirits, depending on where they are on their soul journey.

Spirits contain the personality developed during a life. At the end of each life, they are generally meant to return to connection. There are usually good reasons if they don't. They can learn from the energy that is trapped, whether that energy is positive or negative. Although most spirits pass over peacefully, some who have struggled through life can be unaware or confused and might be ready to receive help from compassionate people like Kelly.

Souls who are lost in the dark night of the soul may refuse to return home. Generally, these souls have been imprinted with particular attitudes and beliefs that made them distrustful, hurt, or angry. They prefer to stay isolated, and it can be a long time before they are ready to return to the higher realms or incarnate again. Stubborn souls have a strong will, and that can be helpful at certain stages of their development, but it can also keep them stuck.

Even after they have made the turnaround, souls may struggle on their journey back to the light. We all have much to learn, whatever our stage of development, but all learning is worthwhile. Nothing is wasted, we are told; every life is valuable. Learning expands us. As humans, our challenging lives play an important part in expanding our universe.

In the next section, we look at different ways souls struggle back toward the higher frequencies.

# SECTION 3: ARISING

# CHAPTER 7

# SOFTENING

Recovery for any lost soul is not possible unless the soul is willing to feel vulnerable. Most people don't like feeling vulnerable, often freezing their emotions to avoid it. The guides devise plans for future lives, designed to pierce through the protective armor souls have created. Sometimes these plans work, and sometimes they backfire.

In this chapter, we explore the past life of a soul who emotionally shuts down after a devastating loss. During the regression, she is presented with an opportunity to redeem her many regrets in an unusual way.

## Avoiding Emotional Pain

All souls like to fulfill the plan for their lives, but sometimes that doesn't happen. Some souls avoid a particular aspect of the plan because a related trauma remains present and influential. When they are ready, however, they can confront and overcome their avoidance. Hedda came to me because she wanted to understand her aversion to having children. In her most recent past life, she refused to have any children, even though being a mother was part of her soul plan. In her current life, she has no children and doesn't want any.

After Hedda enters the trance, I direct her to go through a tunnel into a past life chosen by her guides to illuminate this issue. She reports being stuck.

*This is happening because I don't want to see the truth. Seeing the truth means waking up and feeling pain. I would be confronted with things I don't want to experience. I don't want to see my family die. I don't want to remember it. It was too painful.*

Hedda is hesitant because she senses what is to come. Avoidance has been a pattern in many of her lives.

*I am being told to tell you that I nearly drowned just recently. I got caught in a rip and had to be pulled out. I was not paying attention. That is the pattern of not being in touch with reality—in other words, being asleep. Because I avoid reality, I need brutal experiences to wake me up. I haven't been learning in my lives. I can do it easy or I can do it hard, and I am doing hard because I am pushing away both the pain and what I need to see. I want life to be easy and it just isn't.*

With some gentle coaxing, Hedda decides to move forward slowly.

## Losing Her Mother

She recalls a life as Helga, one of three sisters living in Belgium in the mid-eighteenth century. Their loving parents are wealthy aristocrats. In her late teens, she has withdrawn to a peaceful place near a stream when her father comes to fetch her. Her mother is dying.

*I am a gentle, sensitive person, coming often to this sacred place because it puts me in touch with the happy memories of the times we spent here together as a family. My father knows I am sensitive. Although I am of marrying age, my father is not forcing me to marry. He understands me.*

*Now, Father is holding out his hand, saying gently, "Helga, you need to say goodbye to your mother. You cannot hide down here forever."*

Hedda starts crying softly.

*We go into my mother's bedroom. She has been waiting for me. Looking up, she smiles and holds out her hand, saying, "My lovely girl. I am so proud of you." She calls us all over to the bed. Holding our hands, she looks at us with soft eyes, saying, "Please take care of each other." Her smile shows me she is at peace within herself. Golden light energy fills the room, telling me that spirits are waiting for her. While our father stands beside me stroking Mother's hair, I put my head on her shoulder. My little sister lays her head on Mother's lap as my older sister takes Mother's hand, bringing it up to her cheek. Tears are flowing down our faces.*

*The room seems empty now—her spirit gone, her body hollow. I find comfort remembering the positive, golden energy in the room when she died.*

## Spring and Sunshine Return

Sometime later, Helga's father suggests a suitable husband, whom she accepts.

*It is springtime, and I am going to meet Leon. We are both very happy because we are getting married today. We are listening to the birds singing, and I feel a deep sense of contentment, knowing that Leon feels it too.*

We go to a scene some years after their marriage. Leon and Helga arrive at their new home on the East Coast of North America.

*I see a long drive leading up to a large stone house in the country, not far from the city. My husband is a businessman with ties to various diplomats. He has come in good standing but still has to prove himself to the new republic. We have a little three-year-old daughter, Harriet, whom we call Hattie. I walk around, saying hello to the servants.*

We go to another scene several years later, when Hattie is seven.

# Death and Denial

*I am running toward an overturned carriage on our driveway. Hattie was going to town with Leon. Leon is still inside [the carriage] while Hattie has been thrown out and is lying on the ground, unconscious. The driver jumped clear. I cry for help. Some servants come to help. Gently, they pick up my daughter, carrying her and Leon up to the house. Leon is alive but unconscious. He has been taken to the parlor. He opens his eyes and asks, "How is Hattie?"*

*My daughter is lying on a large stone bench in the kitchen. A few servants are standing around, weeping. One wets cloths with cold water, placing them on Hattie. Her lips are dark pink and her body purple with bruises.*

*The doctor arrives. The servants carry Hattie upstairs into her bedroom. My husband rouses and we climb the stairs together.*

*Although I am nervous and agitated, I focus on helping. I just want it to be over. Part of me knows, looking at my daughter's face, that this is not going to go well, but I refuse to let that thought in.*

*The doctor cuts off her dress, revealing her torso, which is completely purple. Her lips have turned from pink to blue, and yet she looks so peaceful.*

*My husband is sitting in a chair in a corner of the room, his head in his hands, very distressed. He blames himself for the accident because he let her sit up top on the bench with the driver. We both have let her do that many times for the length of the long driveway. She loves the freedom of the wind blowing in her face and hair. We delight in her happiness, just like my parents did with me and my sisters.*

*The doctor is listening to her heart, looking at her swollen body, and shaking his head. The maids are crying softly. My husband's mind is falling apart while I feel a bit removed from it all. The fuss and chaos are too much for me to take in. As I look at my child, I am numb.*

*It is summer and the day is hot. They were going to town for a father and daughter day. She was always so proud walking down the street beside her papa, being such a little miss. When I was with them, walking behind them, I'd watch them chat, pointing out objects of interest to each other. I was so happy seeing them together. Now I am thinking they are never going to do that again.*

Hedda cries inconsolably.

*The doctor comes to me, still shaking his head. He is talking to me, but I cannot hear him anymore because discordant sounds now rush around in my head while, in my mind, I see the indelible image of her little black, swollen body.*

*I put my hand on my husband's knee. He looks at me, crying. We hug each other, and I cry a bit. I know she is still only just alive, and I should go over and hold her, but I cannot move.*

Hedda is weeping.

*I cannot go to her because I feel that, if I never see her dead, she will never be dead. She is our little girl. I know I cannot have any more children, my pregnancy and labor were difficult and there've been several miscarriages. I swallow my pain because there is too much of it to deal with.*

*After the maids dress her little body, I go over and rearrange her dress slightly, but I am switched off. She is something that looks like my daughter rather than actually being my daughter.*

*Now I am standing with my husband watching her coffin go into the ground. I feel so hot, like a stone heated from the hot sun, while he is distraught, crying. I am holding his hand, but I am not as connected to him as I was before. He is like water and I am like a rock. I have hardened, and my heart has turned to stone.*

Hedda cries deeply.

# Glacial Grief

*As I stand by the grave, I think about what I should have done that I didn't do. I should have held my dear little daughter as she died. I should have laid her out and dressed her. I have failed her, and it is such a massive failure. She needed me. She must have been suffering so much pain, her little body thrown into the air and going under the carriage. I am reliving that over and over again, feeling so much remorse with my failure to comfort her.*

Helga is thinking, ruminating, staying in her head and avoiding the pain in her body. There are several reasons why she feels differently about her mother's death compared to her daughter's. Her mother was an adult, her death was not a shock, the passing was beautiful and peaceful, and Helga felt no responsibility for her mother's death.

Hattie died at the beginning of her life, in circumstances that were unexpected and traumatic. Although she did not cause Hattie's death, Helga doesn't feel innocent. As a mother charged with protecting her child, she feels responsible, questioning her decision to let Hattie sit on the top of the carriage with the driver.

Afterward, she reflects on her inability to approach and comfort her daughter. She is unable to forgive herself. Her guilt and self-judgment trap her in a self-perpetuating cycle of despair and isolation, which shuts out her husband and everyone else. Instead of softening, the loss of her daughter resurrects an earlier soul pattern of coping with overwhelming feelings of vulnerability: she freezes her emotions and hardens her heart.

We continue the regression, moving into the future, some years after Hattie has died.

*I am in the kitchen of the same house, but much older. I am sitting at the table and Leon is standing near the window. We still have a lot of love between us, including friendship and companionship, but the light-heartedness is long gone. We never really talk about the loss of our daughter. Whenever he mentions it, I change the subject, saying, "It's in the past now."*

*The only time we visit our daughter's grave together is on her birthday. He takes flowers and talks to her. Other times I go to her graveside alone, but only when I am certain no one is around to disturb me. I stand there with that same disconnected feeling, tidying her gravesite, making sure all is in order. Keeping the grave neat and tidy is important to me, probably because that is all I can do—apart from putting my hand on her gravestone every now and then. I never cry.*

*What I did after her death was as painful to Leon as our daughter's death. He lost me too. He had everything he wanted in life, but he lost the important things: his daughter and his wife.*

*I just went through the motions, doing what had to be done, feeling very little, wearing black—on the inside as well as the outside.*

*He grieved and continued on with his life. I knew he loved me. Previously, his love was so beautiful and warm, cocooned all around me, but after our daughter died, I could only feel it as a warm glow to the side. I couldn't let the love in because my heart had turned to stone.*

We move to another scene in the future.

*We are lying on the bed, both ill and much older. I am going to die in the next few hours, and we are both happy, knowing I will be soon released. This is the closest we have been for a long time. I look at him, telling him I am sorry. He holds my hand saying, "There is no need to be sorry." I think, "That is what I should have done with my daughter, sat there holding her hand." I fade away.*

Helga floats away quickly. She remembers what happened after she died.

*Leon lived on. I didn't visit him because he needed the space he didn't have when I was around. I can see him in his study pinning butterflies to a board, as a collector, having a few quiet, contented years.*

## Replaying to Heal

*I don't feel good about passing. My heart is heavy and full of regret. I feel like I wasted his life, and I have wasted my life too. I wish I could relive my life differently.*

I realize that this is an opportunity for healing. Reliving a past event differently can positively change it in the psyche. I suggest we do that, relive this life in the way she prefers. She agrees. When she replays it, Hedda does so with all the wisdom she has gained from that time up to the present.

*My daughter still dies. She has to die because that is the plan. We are in the room where she is dying. Leon and I are holding onto each other, crying, weeping, both of us in deep grief. I am shuddering as if my life depends on it, managing to stay grounded by desperately hanging on to him. We stay locked together for a long time. I still cannot get my body to stand up and go over there to her.*

I ask Hedda, "What needs to happen for you to be able to do what you really want to do?"

*Now we are back to the doctor arriving. Leon and I are carrying our daughter up the stairs together. I am standing on one side of the bed and my husband is sitting on the other side, holding her hand. Now I am kneeling by her, stroking her hair, holding her hand and saying, "My sweet girl. I love you. I am sorry it is like this." From time to time, I gently kiss her hair.*

*After she dies, Leon and I lovingly bathe her, dress her, and do her hair. I put pink on her cheeks, flowers in her hair and in her hands.*

*She always loved flowers. We take time before burying her. We cry with the doctor, with the servants, and with each other.*

*I don't feel as heavy as I did before, appreciating the power of so many mourning this one little person. So much love is being generated through honoring her that the light comes back in, making it possible for us to even laugh sometimes.*

*Over time, we become more accepting and happier. When she was alive, I would make little floral headbands for my daughter. I keep doing this because it makes me happy. I put them on the heads of little girls who visit. Even a couple of little boys like wearing them. Now, I see a band of these flowers on one of the friendly dogs.*

Hedda laughs.

*Our home becomes a loving household like the one I grew up in. When our faithful servants die, we bury them in the place we buried our daughter. This little graveyard is peaceful and beautiful because we have planted so many flowers there.*

*This time, my husband dies first. We are together on the bed chatting like we always did; he is saying less and less until he finally falls silent. He has a peaceful death.*

*I die several years later surrounded by our servants. They have become my family. At first, I am reluctant to leave the household because I am scared to see my daughter after such a long time.*

I reassure and encourage Hedda to move forward.

*I am walking across a field with the light so bright it is almost blinding. I see shapes across the field. It is my husband and my daughter. We are all young again. Hattie bounds up to me and we hug. We are together again, happy.*

Hedda pauses awhile, taking this all in. Eventually the scene fades away and she moves into her life between lives.

# Suffering and Growth

*I am in a dark, circular room that has two doors opposite each other, each leading to long corridors. On opposite sides of the round room, four large television screens hang on each wall.*

*I come in just as someone arrives from the opposite door. I recognize my current father. We meet frequently in this room and now sit at a table together.*

*He smiles and asks me how I am feeling about this past life with Leon. I am a bit terse and say, "Fine."*

*He says, "You don't want to talk?"*

*I tell him I don't want to go through it again.*

*"Why don't you ever want to learn?" he wonders.*

*I say, "Because it is too hard."*

*He tells me I am very smart and powerful and don't need to fear learning or life.*

*I tell him, "I don't feel smart and powerful; I feel tender and bruised at the end of most lives. I am too sensitive, and it is all too painful."*

*We are looking at each other, and he doesn't know what to do with me. He is calling for help. The spirit I have seen before is here now. I nod at my father who is at the other end of the table, letting him know I am okay. He leaves. I am very private, and I want as few people as possible present now.*

*This guide is a high-level being, and I feel privileged having him with me. He asks me why I am scared. I answer that I don't like to be hurt; all these lives make me extremely tired—the body and the whole experience feels so heavy. He explains why I struggle so much.*

*"You don't let go. You are too hung up on the body. Having a body bothers you. The body is a tool for you to use. You are not the tool. If your saw is rusty, blunt, not cleaned and taken care of properly, it doesn't cut wood very well. You might force it, but it doesn't work.*

*If you look after your saw, clean it, sharpen it, and learn to work with it, it works efficiently and effectively. You always fight your body and the material world. You have no acceptance. You do not stop being a part of the greater cosmic energy that is all life just because you are contained in a physical body. When you deny the body, you separate yourself from the original energy from which you came and to which you will return. In fact, you are always connected. You go through these many lives with their trials and tribulations to be purified so that when you go back, you are refined, pure energy, like a ball of perfect white light."*

*I ask him why we have to go through all of this in the first place. He decides to call in the Great Mother energy to answer. I have met her in my previous sessions.*

*She is asking me if I can hear her because I always seem to have trouble hearing her messages. I know I need to open up so I can take in her wisdom.*

*"What you don't remember, Hedda," she tells me, "is that you were once part of the greater energy. You chose to experience the physical. You need to understand this choice from an expansive perspective. The self that chose to come to earth is the greater self of which you are a part."*

*I am being shown a photo of myself when I was young. It is obvious that I am not the same as I was back then; yet I am a fuller, richer person for the experiences I have had as a youth. As we grow in wisdom, we release what we no longer need, and this changes us. An older person knows what really matters.*

Hedda has been out of balance. Forgetting her spiritual connection, she connected too tightly to the material world. Consequently, she found her earth lives overwhelming. To avoid pain and her feelings of vulnerability, she closed down emotionally, disconnected from herself and others, and used dreams and fantasies to escape.

Losing Hattie in her past life was meant to wake her up. At the time, she pushed back against her pain. But nothing is lost. The real power of that life emerged during Hedda's regression. Her trapped grief was released, and her awareness increased.

By reimagining her daughter's death and allowing herself to grieve fully, Hedda rewrote the history of that past life in her psyche—so much so that years later, she inadvertently referred to the second, happier version of that life as fact.

# Conclusion

Many of us push away our feelings when we suffer great loss. We busy ourselves with work or other activities. We avoid painful topics while ruminating on trivial matters or the views of others. We can become judgmental, depressed, or angry. We inadvertently numb our feelings by tightening various muscles in our body. We refuse to acknowledge our pain, focusing only on the positive, insisting that others have worse tragedies. All these strategies are ways of avoiding feeling vulnerable.

Our journey over many lifetimes is planned to open up our vulnerability. Inevitably, this means experiencing loss. Our bodies are beautifully designed to feel grief. We utilize this brilliant design when we make space for our feelings in our bodies. Grieving is like opening a release valve that lets go of pent-up emotion and resets our psyche, allowing us to go on with our lives. Grieving is painful and takes time, but it is always worthwhile.

Some of us are so shut down or inhibited, we find it difficult to loosen our bodies and cry. If this is the case, we have a challenging choice to make. We can decide to feel and release our distressing emotions. We can ask for help from our spirit guides and others, if that feels right. Now, we focus on what we have lost, acknowledging how painful it is. To do this, we need to let go of our old programing that we heard so often when we were young: "Stop feeling sorry for yourself!" Remember, for everything there is a season, and that includes a time to weep. Whenever a thought, a memory, a familiar place or event upsets you, open the door wide to let your grief in, knowing that it will leave once you have acknowledged it fully by weeping, breathing deeply, or just allowing yourself to feel sad.

Depression is the avoidance of hurt and anger, while active sadness allows us to express what we have lost.

# CHAPTER 8
# EMERGING

Souls who have felt extremely alone and separate often struggle to find their way back to peace and love. Many play out their karma in lives of suffering and victimization. This is confusing for them. Some spend lifetimes bouncing back and forth between being victims and perpetrators. Emerging from these patterns is a struggle.

Souls who have suffered the devastating consequences of their decisions can lose trust in their choices. They begin to procrastinate, trying to avoid making the wrong choice. In reality, refusing to choose is still a choice, one with adverse consequences. These souls end up desperately reacting to circumstances that they have inadvertently created.

In this chapter, we hear the stories of three souls who failed to think through the decisions they made in their past lives. In their current lives, they are finding their way back to connection, worthiness, and better decision-making. They have rich crops of experience to reap on this journey.

## Overwhelming Loss

Although only in her twenties, Kahlia has already experienced more than her share of grief. Eight months earlier, her husband had been killed in a motorcycle accident. Her grandpop had been killed nine years previously in a car crash, and her sister had drowned during a family holiday. She had also lost pets under tragic circumstances— her dog had been run over, and her horse had to be put down after breaking its leg during a storm. Kahlia also experienced a miscarriage before her son, now one year old, was born. Still mourning the loss of her beloved husband, Kahlia wanted to make sense of these tragedies and clear any blocks to understanding her life's purpose.

*During her regression, she recalls a number of significant lives. In her early incarnations, she was peaceful and vulnerable. Then, as a child of twelve, she is standing on the edge of a cobblestone street, watching a horse and cart pass by. Someone grabs her from behind, ties a sack around her head, and throws her onto the cart. Along with many others, she is transported to a castle, where a crowd has gathered to watch them mount the scaffold. Kahlia and the others are impaled, then burned to death. Connecting with the young girl's feelings, Kahlia struggles with the unfairness of it all.*

*The young girl was the epitome of innocence. She felt hurt, sadness, and unfairness. She didn't have time to grow any anger. I had that life to wake up to the dark side of humanity.*

*The people who did this were in authority. They were scared too. They did it to prove a point—to frighten others. I don't think I was a witch, but I may have been linked to others who were accused of witchcraft.*

After this brutal execution, Kahlia's soul begins to shut down emotionally. Subsequently, her soul incarnates as an Egyptian seer, whose clairvoyant powers come from his nonphysical connections. Still, a sense of repressed sadness carries over from the little girl's life, numbing the seer's emotions. He uses his powers to help and heal people but takes as much as he gives. Depressed and lacking vitality, he trades in gossip, betraying his clients' confidences. Kahlia shares the seer's thoughts.

*I know what is on the other side, and I have no fear of death. I am bored with earth.*

*I am a good person for many people. From helping them I am known, respected, and important. But I push the boundaries, admiring myself and getting admiration from others. I feel it, and it feeds me. I feel better than others, above them.*

Jealous of his success, the seer's brother reports him to the authorities. They invade and ransack his house before strangling him. Kahlia tells me how the seer responds.

*My brother wasted my life. I am still angry about being betrayed and strangled. I wasn't angry until then.*

The seer's anger shapes this soul's subsequent incarnations. No longer the victim, he slides deeper and deeper into violence.

*They are showing me lots of lives. I am torturing prisoners in a castle. I am taking my self-hate out on these people. I am so angry. I can feel the rage pulsing inside me. I am trying to kill the hurt in myself by killing others, externalizing what I feel inside. It's like I am trying to get it out of myself.*

Then something happens that changes the dynamic. Kahlia is given images of a woman who lived in Arizona in the nineteenth century.

*She is striding through a barren landscape beside a railway line. It is like she is on a mission, and yet there is nowhere for her to go. There is an old western-style town a hundred yards to her right, but she just passes on by. She is walking to somewhere and away from something. She doesn't want to go back to what happened. There is an ache in my heart.*

From experience, I realize this woman has died and her spirit is lost. I ask Kahlia to breathe through the ache in her heart. After she feels calm, I suggest she move forward with the woman while continuing to breathe, slowly and deeply, through any emotion that surfaces. Kahlia shares the information she is receiving.

*She lost everything—her child and her husband. I am full of anger. My husband got us into this situation, and he died violently. This is a lawless place, full of ongoing retaliation, squabbles requiring revenge. I don't want to play this game. My husband killed one of them, then they came for us. They killed him, killed the baby, and then they took me. I am fighting them. They sexually assault me. I see them break my neck, but there is something in me that is still alive.*

The spirit of this woman speaks in the first person, while the descriptive third person comes from Kahlia's higher perspective.

*She is on the railway track, screaming in anger. She has no room for sadness because she is so angry. She is furious, wanting to avenge the loss. She was like that before. She was very bossy and strong and told him what to do. She was an angry person.*

I note that this woman blames her husband for the payback when speaking in first person. Soon after, Kahlia explains that the woman was bossy and told him what to do. This is an example of a spirit carrying over faulty beliefs. Because of the awful consequences of her husband's actions, she has shifted the blame. This is common and tricky to deal with. Because Kahlia is aware of the truth, I ignore this discrepancy.

Some clients, afraid of feeling shame, can resist widening their perspective and seeing the truth, even though this would lead them to the change they desire. Shifting their perspective takes a delicate touch and cautious questioning.

To clear the anger from our past lives, I explain, we need to love and accept all parts of ourselves, including those that have taken the most evil of actions. Taking a deep breath, Kahlia agrees. I ask how she feels now about the Egyptian life. She sees how the seer created his death by overstepping the boundaries.

*The Egyptian man was knowledgeable and wise but pushed the boundaries of what was permitted at the time. He was feeding off the ego boost he got from helping people.*

Viewing that past life from the larger perspective of Kahlia's soul dissipates the seer's anger. Then we move to the life of the torturer.

*I knew in doing the torture it was my own sadness, but that wasn't enough to stop me. I felt compelled, and I didn't know how to get out of it. In that life, I died with an axe in the back of the head. There was nothingness. There is heaviness on me. Now I see him sitting in darkness and nothingness. It is his own prison of guilt and self-hate.*

I make a suggestion to help Kahlia release him.

"You know how he feels. Send him love and light until you get his attention. Now, tell him how much you appreciate him teaching you and your larger self what it is like to hate so deeply. Life is about experience and knowing that is useful." Kahlia is happy to oblige.

*He likes being acknowledged. I am helping him, but he is timid about coming out.*

I suggest he might like to go to a healing place to be restored.

*The guides are there now, and he is going with them.*

Knowing the torturer is safe and being cared for, we move on to the angry woman in Arizona. Kahlia explains how she feels.

*I feel sad for her. Compassion. She was a strong woman but got caught up in wrong actions. That knowledge is useful. She has her head down and feels sad. She needs forgiveness.*

I make a suggestion. "Send her love and light. Once you have her attention, thank her for teaching you and others about getting off track with strength."

It doesn't take long before Kahlia tells me the western woman has gone now. She, too, is being restored.

Kahlia wants to know why her husband passed over so young. She easily connects with him and explains what she receives.

*In our previous past life together, I was the unsympathetic man who was emotionally shut down. He was the wife grieving the loss of her baby.*

*The birth of the baby was difficult, and it seemed that one of them would die. The woman regretted that the baby died. She was distraught that the baby had suffered and missed out on life. He just said that dying in his current life was karmic. It was about realizing that dying is not traumatic. The baby didn't suffer.*

*Losing him this life is balancing my karma too. In that past life, I was unsympathetic, grumpy, arrogant, rigid, and old-fashioned regarding the gender division of labor. I was actually a bit of a pig.*

Kahlia was satisfied with the explanation she received from her husband, realizing all happened for their highest good.

At the beginning of our session, I had asked Kahlia if she had shut down in her current life. She said she had been struggling to express traumatic emotion. Now, at the end of her session, she feels drained but much lighter, knowing she has released a great deal of grief and anger. Now, she wishes to know about her future. She is given a glimpse of her next life.

*I see a tropical beach. It is peaceful. I am walking on the beach with two children beside me. I am around thirty-seven to forty and content in my body. I am short in height and my hair is dark. Being shorter is about developing wisdom, not feeling above others. I am quieter in myself. I am ultra easy-going, taking things as they come. I am in the flow and connected to my higher self.*

*There are bumps on the road. I see that my parents die around that time, and I am sad. I have a husband and the relationship is positive.*

*We are like-minded and confident with each other. We own some sort of wellness place. It is peaceful and fulfilling. I am very content. Clients come from everywhere. My purpose is building inner strength and healthy humility.*

Kahlia has taken a long, tough journey through her many lives. She went from innocence to injustice, betrayal, hate, and anger before emerging with experiences of loss, victimization, and humiliation. Finally, she began opening up to vulnerability, compassion, humility, and love.

In her violent past lives, Kahlia's soul had overridden any hint of vulnerability with the energy of hate and anger. This hardened her heart. During the regression, she felt her heart ache. This time, instead of running away from the pain, she gave it space.

Facing what we have done in the past and feeling the vulnerability we disowned helps us build inner strength and healthy humility. By welcoming all her lost past life personalities—the angry, the vengeful, and the shameful—with compassion and gratitude, Kahlia restored their inner peace, continuing the process of emerging from the darkness.

## Making a Clean Cut

Scott has been stuck for many lifetimes. His Council of Elders, who appear during a regression, includes a wizard. The wizard is sitting with his clasped hands resting on a table. Scott asks about his soul lessons and reports the wizard's response.

*He is not angry, but he is questioning me. "Haven't you learned from this already?" he demands, because I have done the same thing many times. I have been stuck. Before I came to this past life, I was ashamed that I hadn't learned.*

Scott has been indecisive. The word "decision" comes from the Latin "decisio," meaning "to cut." Being decisive means making a clear choice—taking one option while leaving the other behind. When faced with a choice in the past life, Scott wanted to implement both options. In his current life, he was struggling with the same dilemma.

In the past life, he is a deckhand on a galleon captained by his father. Scott is pushed into a barrel and thrown overboard.

*I was pushed by a man with a beard. I was one of the crew; he was jealous of me. He wasn't the captain but higher than the crew. I was a deckhand. I had influence with others.*

I ask questions to help Scott find out what happened. This is not easy because several times during our investigation of this past life, Scott avoids taking responsibility for the decisions he made before the ship left port and those he subsequently made on board. Instead, he washes his hands of any wrongdoing. This is his first report of what happened:

*The bearded man was doing his job to protect the crew. I tried to take over. The captain was dead. The crew poisoned him. The man with the beard told the crew the captain was dead and that he was taking over. It was mutiny.*

*He was a kind captain. He had a wig with a ponytail and wore a blue velvet jacket with gold on the seams. I see him with a telescope.*

*That life was about justice. I tried to put things right.*

I ask Scott to check with the wizard. The wizard insists that Scott must work it out for himself.

*The captain was my father. I was really angry [after the mutiny]. I think I killed most of the crew. I killed all the other deckhands in one go with an axe. I was strong. The man with the beard hit me from behind while I was killing these four men, two my age and two older. We all wore the same dirty cream clothes. They were not strong enough to listen and see what was going on. They were weak. What I did was in the best interests of everyone involved. I didn't take sides until they poisoned the captain. For me, they went to the point of no return.*

Scott's story doesn't quite add up. If the captain was kind, why would the bearded man poison him and mutiny? Scott tries again to explain what happened.

*I could have sorted this before my father was killed by talking to him. I could have told him what I was observing in the crew. We were in trouble. The sail was broken; we were in hot weather and short of water. I couldn't talk to him. He wouldn't listen to me.*

*I think the captain thought I hadn't secured the sail. It wasn't me. It was the man with the beard. He didn't like me telling on him.*

*Oh! I just heard the guides say, "You didn't do your job properly."*

It turns out that Scott is still avoiding the truth. I ask what "not doing your job properly" means.

*An image just popped in. I am beneath the deck, drinking and playing cards with the crew. I have four diamonds [playing cards] in my hand while I am leaning on the barrel, feeling its ridges under my arms. Storage space is at the bottom of the ship and filled with grain. We are transporting that somewhere because that is what the ship does.*

*Now, I keep seeing a girl on the middle deck. I brought her on and I wasn't supposed to. While we were playing cards, she was discovered. No one knew until then. She is my younger sister. She wanted to see what we did. She should have been home with our two older brothers and mother on the farm. We are Dutch. I would have done anything for her. She twisted my arm.*

I ask for more information about this sister. The story suddenly changes again.

*I told them she was my sister. She wasn't my sister. She is looking at me in a very desiring way. She makes me feel good, and I don't want to be on the ship away from her. I was supposed to be following*

155

*the family line. When she was discovered, it caused a lot of problems with the crew. The captain found out and was angry.*

The real story now comes out. Scott hid the girl as a stowaway. He decided he could follow the family line—keeping his father happy and meeting his sexual desires as well. As for the untied sail, he was the one who had not secured the sail properly. The crew expected the captain to severely punish the deckhand's serious transgressions, which had put their lives at risk, but the captain didn't. The bearded man and the crew mutinied. They poisoned the captain and eventually threw Scott overboard.

When Scott came to the regression, he was in a similar situation. He'd been planning to go home to England to spend time with his father, but recently he had fallen for a girl and didn't want to leave.

The regression helped Scott see the pattern of his poor decisions. Afterward, he left Australia and returned home. The regression also helped him overcome his dreadful fear of dark ocean water. His spirit had been stuck in the depths since he'd been thrown overboard hundreds of years before.

Finally, Scott faced what he'd done, realizing he would be better served by making clear decisions and taking responsibility for his choices, even when that meant others were unhappy.

His struggle with being truthful came from a fear of being punished for doing the wrong thing. Being thrown overboard so suddenly was extremely traumatic. His reluctance to admit his guilt, even to himself, is understandable. It is a naïve way of hiding from the truth. Scott thought if he didn't see it, it didn't count.

Retreating from guilt is common in many of us, but hiding from the truth does not benefit us in the long term. We end up feeling like fakes—which, to varying degrees, we are.

# Growing Up the Party Girl

Tiffany is another example of this challenging road back to positivity. Her life is a mess, and she comes to see me, hoping to discover why. Although she is now married, she still feels unsettled, jealous, insecure, and worthless. She has suffered a number of health problems and addictions and is on medication for bipolar disorder. Before we begin her regression, she describes how she feels.

*I've felt unloved by my whole family. I put them through a lot of shit when I was in my teens and twenties by using drugs and alcohol. I expect people to be their best, and I get disappointed when they turn out to be selfish, irresponsible, and incompetent.*

*I yell at them, trying to get them to understand, but they think I am just being nasty. Maybe I am being nasty. I am coming from a very dark place. I feel small, like I am worthless and don't belong in the family. I don't deserve them.*

*They don't love me because I am not good enough. I can't imagine loving this girl I am either. She is horrible, negative, and selfish. I have incredible self-doubt, and I feel incredibly intimidated by strong, loving, and competent people.*

*I feel a very deep sadness. I just don't want to be here anymore.*

Tiffany wants to understand her anger, disappointment, and self-doubt. Once she is relaxed and ready, she accesses a past life. She is a girl living on a ranch in North America.

*I love the horses, and I want to ride. I take off my apron and jump on a chestnut brown horse. We are riding through the forest, through the pine trees. It is beautiful, and I feel good. I am riding barefoot and bareback. I often do this, riding by myself. It gives me a sense of freedom.*

*My name is Molly. I am in my late twenties and single. I grew up here. My family owned this place.*

*I trap rabbits and there is a vegetable garden. I feed the chickens, cook, and tend the fireplace. It gets cold here in the winter. I am alone. I did have parents who lived here, but they went away. I feel free living here alone.*

I ask if she knows when her parents left.

*I see a man, a big fat man. I don't like him. I think he is related to me. He died. I killed him, stabbed him in his big fat stomach. He was on top of me. He deserved it. It took a while for him to die. He was shocked. I ran out of the house and jumped on my horse.*

*He was much older than me. I think he was my father. He abused me since I was little. My mother died when I was a teenager, but he abused me before that. He abused her too. I just feel relieved to be free of him.*

We go to the last day of Molly's life.

*I am at the ranch, alone. I am much older, in my late sixties. I have survived here by myself. It has been a peaceful life since he has gone. I am ready to go. I am in my wooden rocking chair. I just let go quietly.*

Molly passes over peacefully, meeting her guide in her life between lives.

*I sense he has long grey hair, a beard, and kind, wrinkled eyes. I can't see him, but I feel him.*

The guide now tries to help Tiffany understand the path she has been taking.

*I think there is a block. I think I am supposed to figure it out for myself. He says it is because I don't want to hear. I guess that's true. I am afraid I am wrong and will never get it right. I have had many lives where I have been stuck. I think I am afraid of what I will have to do if I do see it. I would have to stop being unhappy and work on enjoying life. I would have to take responsibility for the way I feel and stop blaming everyone else and life itself. I have had a lot of hard, challenging lives that have worn me down. I am always a victim.*

I check, asking Tiffany if she was always a victim in her earth lives.

*No. I just got a sense of darkness. The dark path is awful. It is horrible carrying hatred. I had several lives like that. I want to push it all away. If I didn't have those lives, I wouldn't be able to see the light. The light would be meaningless.*

*The guide is pointing something out on a scroll. It is that I have not been taking responsibility for the way I feel. I make myself into a victim all the time. It makes life easier because I don't have to be anything. I can drift. Problem is, I am never really happy. I point at other people and point at my life circumstances and feel negative about them rather than looking at myself.*

*I hate the idea of being a perpetrator. I think I would rather be hurt than let other people be hurt.*

*I see my own negativity and uselessness in life, and I can't tolerate it, just like someone who gives up smoking and then hates everyone who smokes.*

*I am going to let it go and live in the light. I can give up my negativity and accept that negativity is other people's path at this point. They don't have to be like me, agree with me, and do what I do.*

*I want to go to the Council of Elders. Now I am surrounded by them, saying hello and thanking them. They are smiling and nodding. I am receiving love and acceptance.*

The Council of Elders answers her questions. She wonders why she doesn't like being on earth.

*On earth I always felt I was being trapped in negativity, the dou-ble-edged sword, perpetrator or victim. But I don't have to live like that anymore. I need to let go and love.*

She wants to know why she is so afraid of being alone. She receives the answers.

*Because of all the sadness and negativity, I feared doing something to myself. I needed all the people around to distract me from not want-ing to live. The instant gratification of partying with drugs and alcohol fed me. When no one was around, I had no one to play victim to and no one to blame. All I wanted to do was party. People would hang around me because I was fun. But I was pretending. No one sus-pected that I was sad inside. I did try to kill myself a few times when I was with different groups of people. They were surprised. Somehow, I pulled myself together and kept going.*

Tiffany wants to know why she has so many issues with chil-dren. She has never wanted to have children and doesn't like being around them. But she has a stepson, Hunter, aged fifteen, who she describes as a "sweet little boy." Still, she is annoyed with having a child in her life.

*Hunter is in my life to help me master the irritation and disappoint-ment I feel toward people. I am to learn to love the fifteen-year-old. Looking at Hunter now, I can see he is just like me. He needs uncon-ditional love and stability. I can definitely give it to him if I get over my neediness. It feels like I have another person between me and my husband, and I think my husband loves Hunter more than me. I have been saying I always feel last in the family.*

I ask Tiffany where that comes from. She is thoughtful for a few moments.

*My family of origin.*

Tiffany felt she came last in her first family, and now she feels the same in the family she has created as an adult. I ask her how it feels to come last. She weeps deeply for several minutes.

*It's not them that puts me last, it is me who puts me last. My husband is actually afraid Hunter might choose his mother over him. I didn't like Hunter being around because he reminds me of me. I think he is pretty unhappy. I can make a difference in my stepson's life. I understand him, and I can be loving and accepting. My husband needs help to manage his son. I am to see my husband and me as the parents and Hunter as the child. The stability of the family comes from the parents. Hunter is the child, not me.*

Tiffany wonders how she can release her blocks.

*They are saying I am to just take a deep breath and think about what I am feeling. I am to look to see where the feeling is coming from. I don't need to take it on board. I need to let it go. Most of the time, it is irrational and has nothing to do with me.*

She wants to know how to get rid of self-doubt, insecurities, guilt, and unworthiness.

*If I learn to love unconditionally, then that will automatically replace the other negative feelings. I need to stop fighting with myself. I am to practice accepting others and accepting myself and just be.*

*My life purpose is to learn to be giving and loving. I am on the right track, but I need to laugh more, be happy, and let go of negativity, irritation, and intolerance. I will be happier when I am more accepting of others.*

After the session, Tiffany feels different and sees the close relationship between a victim and a perpetrator.

*The perpetrator and victim thing is interesting. I can see both sides now, and I struggle to pick a side. I can see there is no right or wrong.*

Tiffany has been trying to get herself together. She admits she has given her friends and family hell with her use of drugs and alcohol. She has been negative and jealous, even of her pleasant stepson.

She knows she's been down the dark path in her past lives and no longer wants to hurt people as she has previously. In spite of this, she was still hurting others. And she was hurting herself too. She hadn't completely let go of the old pattern of protecting herself by pushing people away and using various distractions to avoid taking responsibility for herself and her future. She didn't know how to protect herself in a healthy way.

As Molly, she took responsibility for her life, killing her rapist father. Although this gave her a life of peace and happiness, she didn't feel good about the way she achieved it. She gave up her power and became a victim in many subsequent lifetimes.

Her feelings of inadequacy and helplessness were still present in her current life. Until she came for the regression, she was giving in to these feelings. She had a choice: to take responsibility for her happiness or continue brooding and feeling sorry for herself. Once she could clearly see how she was hurting herself as well as others, she made her choice. Now, she is focused on reclaiming her power and responsibility.

Although this knowledge might be hard to face, being a victim is a choice. Most people who feel like victims don't realize this. Like Tiffany, they are caught in shortsighted actions that temporarily alleviate their pain, while creating more stress and problems in the long-term.

When we are struggling in life, stopping to take stock and seeking help to unravel our problems is the first step in the right direction. Seeing a way forward is the next step. The third step is implementing the needed changes. In reality, shifting from victimhood to personal empowerment is like ascending a staircase.

We need to keep taking each step purposefully and carefully while being kind to ourselves and others.

## Conclusion

Many of our problems in life come from avoiding responsibility. When we are emerging from dark lives as perpetrators, we sense that we have misused our power. Power and responsibility go together. Because we fear misusing our power, we shun responsibility. We would rather leave the power with others. But renouncing our power leads to feelings of powerlessness. Some of us tend to complain when those with power don't exercise it in the way we prefer. Much of our current dissatisfaction with politics is rooted in our refusal to take responsibility for our own lives. It is often more comfortable just to blame.

When blaming or criticizing others, check to see if you avoid stepping out of your comfort zone. Do you fear making mistakes, not fulfilling your obligations, or misusing your power? Critiquing the behavior of others can be useful. How would you use their power? How can you stay humble while exercising power? What do you need to change in order to trust yourself with responsibility and power? Becoming more aware is always the beginning of making a change.

# CHAPTER 9
# LEARNING TO LOVE

On the journey back to our true selves, we experience challenges designed to wake us up to the power of love. Closing ourselves off to love means closing ourselves off to our higher guidance. It is a relief to know we are loved and being guided.

Our first task is to love ourselves. I have noticed some people glibly say that they love themselves, only to engage in self-flagellation or denigrate others. Self-love is not a Facebook meme. Self-love means accepting all aspects of ourselves—not just the façade we present to the world. Most of us have disowned some of our past behaviors, which means disowning some of our past selves. Indeed, when we criticize others, we are usually responding to an unacknowledged aspect of our soul's history. People who practice genuine self-love have no need to castigate others.

Self-love, then, is only for the strong. Souls who face their demons, discovering that they've been mean, careless, selfish, controlling, or violent in their relationships, undertake a grueling journey back to self-forgiveness and love.

We have seen in earlier chapters how souls can disown their vulnerability. We can also disown our anger. Although we are focused on our past lives in this book, we can push away these emotions in our current lives as well. We love ourselves when every lost part is found, accepted, and treated with grace. Grace means being grateful for the lessons our past selves have taught us, no matter what their behavior. It is easy to discern once we have learnt how to carry ourselves in the world, but who taught us?

Our younger, naïve selves. How precious are these lessons that help us grow in wisdom? How brave and deserving of acknowledgement are these earlier iterations of ourselves?

Let's begin with another story from Rachel, the mercenary you met in chapter 5. As you might imagine, Rachel's soul endured a long and treacherous journey back to connection. Here's a past life in which she experienced different dimensions of love—and learned the difference between passion and enduring love.

## Enduring Love

There are many different kinds of love. For many of us, romantic, passionate love—or eros—is the highest form of love. We experience a total connection with our lover, a feeling of wholeness. Unfortunately, this sense of connection is often fueled by fantasy rather than reality.

When we are needy, we can latch on to our lover in a compulsive and immature way. Our sexual and emotional energies are likely to be unbalanced. These relationships can consume us, like a bushfire raging out of control.

Rachel, during one of her regressions, experiences this passion in one of her past lives as a woman called Tani. Her husband is one of two primary romantic soulmates with whom she incarnates during her hundreds of lives.

*I am in a desert in Africa, living as part of a group whose people have red mud in their hair. I see mud huts, blankets, and a lone tree in the distance. The red soil is hard and dry with cracks in it.*

*I am just standing, catching a bit of a breeze, while people are milling about. I am waiting for my husband. He comes out of the hut and puts his arm around my shoulder. He has a really nice energy.*

*I am a female in my mid-twenties, and we have a couple of little children. We are in love, which is good, because marriages in this com-*

*munity are arranged. We are walking toward the lonely tree, talking with each other. At the tree, we are touching and kissing and enjoying being with each other. We are in a little love bubble. It is a bit of an issue in the village that we are so caught up with each other. We spend our life together whereas the others do not. The men are with men and the women with women. We are focused on each other and pay little attention to our children.*

*An elder is coming over. He is annoyed and tells us to come back to the village. This elder is my husband's grandfather. We walk back and the older men and women of the village are going on about our behavior, berating us. We are told that it is unbecoming to both of us. I am emasculating him, and he is allowing it to happen.*

*We tell them we love each other. They say that doesn't matter. The group is communal, and we are not acting communally. They are saying if we cannot behave appropriately, they will make it so we have to. My husband is saying they can't break our bond, as us being together makes everyone stronger. They disagree.*

*Now an old man is shaking his head, saying we have to divorce and marry other people. We are not happy.*

*I am crying, saying, "No, no!" I look to my mother for help, but she turns and waves me away. My father is not interested either. I am looking for sympathy from anyone, and no one is giving it to me, although no one is rejecting me or disliking me. They are just focused on the good of all. To survive, we need to look out for each other. My husband is arguing, saying, "She is mine. She is my wife; you can't take her."*

*An elder says, "It is done. You are divorced. Other marriages will be arranged." My husband is still protesting as we are being separated and I am being taken away.*

*I am in a women's communal hut, lying on the floor, crying. My children come up, and I say it is okay and hold them, seeing him in them.*

*Now some women come and gently take the children elsewhere. We are going to do a cleansing ritual. They take off my jewelry and clothes. We are sitting on mats on the ground, and the women are compassionately bathing me. My mother is talking soothingly to me, suggesting I think about the community.*

*I sleep in the big hut while our marriage hut is being cleaned and given to others. I know I can't go back there.*

*Now it is sometime later, and I am getting married again. I am not as depressed as I was, but I am certainly not happy. I have been instructed a lot about being kind to my new husband. He has been chosen well. He is a little younger than me and happy to have me. I can still have children. I recognize his soul. He is soul-related to me in some way.*

*We have a ritual ceremony. I come around. My new husband is nice and good-looking. We really believe in ritual cleansing, which seems to shift our energy. We have a big party after the ceremony. We have our wedding night, and I get pregnant.*

*My ex-husband is already remarried to a younger woman. I see them across the way. He is okay.*

*I am at peace with my new husband, companionable with him, even though I am not as attached as I was with my previous husband. I have a better relationship with my children too, paying more attention to them now.*

*My ex-husband and I don't have much to do with each other. Genders don't mix much, especially when not married. Women have women's business and men have men's business. Afterward, our previous behavior is not held against us.*

*I have adjusted, and I am fine. There is a peace in this new relationship that I didn't have with my previous husband. Because the obsession we shared was taboo, I felt unsettled before. Despite all that passion, I was in a dream world, not really living. A lot of people think* living is having all these strong emotions. It isn't. Living is peaceful. There is no place for extreme emotions like passion. True living is being on your path. Now, I have the mental space and energy to participate in the community. I have more friends. I am more balanced.

I didn't engage in any jealousy. After a lot of grief, I accepted the situation and let go of the old relationship, welcoming the new. Then I got on with life.

Later, I look back at my first husband with fondness, but I shake my head a little bit, thinking of the follies of youth, that strong, all-consuming connection and sexual attraction we shared. I forgive myself for that earlier madness.

In old age, he and I are able to speak impartially to each other, friendly and polite, pleased for each other's happiness.

At the end of my life, I am in a hut that is quite smoky. People are with me, mainly women, and also the elders observing our customs. The men I married are already dead. I am old. I have children, grandchildren, and great-grandchildren. My hair is white, and my boobs are really saggy. I am okay. It doesn't feel like the end, just another stage of life. I have no attachment to anything, no resentment or regrets. I have lived a long life, a good life.

My breathing is getting shallower. At my last breath, the singing changes to help my spirit push up. I move up into a tunnel of light. I am disappearing because we believe we go back into the ether. It is like all the specifics of that life are dissolving around me and only my spirit continues.

My guide meets me right at the top. He looks very happy. He says, "Well done." My eternal mother is there, giving me a hug. She says, "It was a great life."

Having been born into a community with strictly defined gender roles and a tradition of arranged marriages, Tani's passion for her first husband threatened to tear the social fabric apart.

There was no room for the intense romantic obsession this couple shared. This may seem strange in our current culture, where eros is celebrated and greatly desired. But Rachel's past life demonstrates the limits of an all-consuming love. It is out of balance.

By the standards of their community, Tani and her husband were living selfishly. They put their sexual passion ahead of the needs of their children, their families, and the broader group. Their mutual passion led them to neglect their children. They were unaware of their responsibilities as adults. The elders in the community could not allow this to continue.

Tani's second marriage offered her the chance to experience a quieter, more enduring kind of love. Because this love was calmer and more balanced, she formed loving familial bonds with her children, grandchildren, and great-grandchildren. Ironically, this is the kind of love she would have shared with her first husband after the fires of eros died down within them both. We cannot sustain such an intense love for a lifetime. And if we could, we would miss out on the mature enduring love and the rich familial love, which we ultimately find to be fulfilling.

Eros presents another danger. It is like putting all our eggs in one basket. If our beloved dies, we are left bereft. We have taken out no emotional insurance for that eventuality because we haven't opened ourselves to the nurturing love of our family and friends.

Tani's community used rituals to help shift misplaced energy. She was emotionally distraught after being separated from her first husband, but the women calmed her with their compassion and cleansing rituals. Rituals are important for humans. They help us come to terms with change, especially changes that are sudden, painful, and wrenching. They are a way of helping us move on.

Balancing our love for others with our love for ourselves is also a fundamental goal of our soul development. We don't graduate from the earth school until we can live this balance. In some lives, we are given the opportunity to begin developing qualities such as self-sacrifice and self-discipline, qualities we need to experience and refine as we continue our journey on earth. After being forced to give up her first husband, Tani began to develop these deeper qualities within her soul.

Life is less a struggle and more joyful when we have integrated the past selves that we previously disowned. Only then can we truly express love. In the next two cases, we explore the journey of two souls reconnecting with their past and finding genuine love—love for themselves and love for others.

## Surfacing Anger

Mila, an unemployed counsellor, has a lot of problems. Her marriage fell apart due to her husband's extramarital affairs. She felt compelled to leave the city where her ex-husband still lived, even though it meant walking away from her business. Not only is Mila struggling financially, she is missing her dogs, which had to stay behind with her husband. She doesn't know if she will ever get them back. Overall, Mila feels afraid and unhappy, as if she is being punished for some unknown wrongdoing.

During her session, she relives the life of a young girl who feels uncomfortable around angry people. As a young adult, she decides she won't be angry like them.

*I am just going to be nice to people all the time and appreciate them. If they think I am simple, I'll ignore it. Sometimes it hurts because they might yell at me.*

She is determined to be happy but struggles to be patient.

*Sometimes I get annoyed with them and say, "Stop hassling me!" They don't like it when I am annoyed, and they don't like it when I am happy. I don't fit in.*

She eventually leaves the town and lives in a cave, befriending the native animals and eating berries. These don't sustain her, and soon she passes over. She reflects on this life.

*I am very proud of who I was: adventurous, brave, different, and true to myself. I was in the right place for me, and others were in an angry place.*

*I was trying to be what people wanted so they would want to be with me. It was never going to work. They need insight into who they really are. They think anger is who they really are and believe that letting it go will be scary.*

This realization triggers something in Mila. She suddenly starts feeling uncomfortably warm while sitting in the chair in my room. I turn down the thermostat on the air conditioner, but it doesn't help.

*I am very hot. There is a burning hole in my front torso, from my throat to my stomach. It is like a volcano: smoldering, black, red, and steamy like hot, heavy rocks.*

*It is anger. All my body is upset, all my organs, very annoyed. Furious!*

*I can't make things happen. I feel annoyed even saying the word "can't." It is rebelling against not doing what is right for me. Everyone wants a piece of me. I don't even know who I am. It is like I betrayed myself all along in my current life.*

In her current life, Mila was sent to boarding school, where she rebelled against the restrictions imposed on her. Eventually, she settled down and made the best of it, but she knows the person she pretended to be wasn't her true self.

As an adult, she trusted her husband, who lied and betrayed her. She forgave him, but the next time he cheated, he left her. She asks her guides the reason for her anger.

*Betrayal. I have been betraying myself, and I have been betrayed. I need to honor myself more. Being betrayed is not my problem.*

She realizes the depth of her repressed anger, which was even present in her past life as the misunderstood young girl. She wants to know why anger is part of our makeup.

*Anger is there to help us survive physically. People use anger to feel safe. They feel safe, alive, and authentic when they are angry. You can treat the anger with gentleness, tell it it's okay, love it, and embrace it; then it can relax and feel loved.*

*I do feel like I have been a bit of rag on the floor that people wiped their feet on. I lost who I was while my husband was having an affair and lying to me. I suspected it and asked him. He lied. I trusted him instead of trusting my own intuition. I betrayed myself.*

*The anger is cooling down now.*

Mila has had a pattern of disowning her anger in her recent past lives. Sometime during her soul journey back to connection, she decided anger was wrong and dangerous, so she should avoid it in herself and in others.

In the past life, the young girl was affected by the anger of others and did her best to be positive. In truth, she just buried her anger and projected it onto others, seeing their anger while denying her own. In her current life, Mila felt angry at her husband's behavior. Again, she tried to manage her anger by repressing it. But repression doesn't really work. It is a form of self-betrayal and self-judgment. Mila had split herself into two halves, believing the calm half was good while the angry half was bad. She tried to reject the bad part and failed. We cannot love ourselves when we have rejected anger. Anger is a natural human emotion. We need to accept and understand our anger. It is always informative, with the potential to teach us more about ourselves and others.

Once Mila accepted her anger, she could move on.

*I have to be very kind, strong-minded, and focused. I must not lose sight now of what I have to do. I need to hang on.*

*It is very white here. I am aware of three people in light robes, and the four of us are sitting on the floor. They are saying, "Why are you stuck in your current life and not moving on as planned?"*

As Mila doesn't know the answer, I suggest she ask them to remind her of the plan.

*They are laughing, telling me I should be having a better time and having fun. That was the plan. My marriage ended to help me focus on who I am, so I don't need permission to be myself. I have to do things for myself and not rely on other people. I haven't trusted myself and my ability to take action. I haven't liked myself. This marriage breakup had to happen for me to like myself. They are saying, "Stop moaning; have fun and count your blessings. More will come when you do this. In the field, horses can just be. They are more than happy." I am to internalize that and just be.*

Mila sees an image of soup with all different vegetables, some that she likes and some that she dislikes. She is in the soup, emerging with the bits falling away.

*I need to appreciate the soup for nurturing me. I am only just now getting out of the soup. My guides are washing it off me. It has been very heavy and thick, and now I feel light. It is a challenge to not fall back into the soup. I have to focus on being—not doing, not striving, just being authentic to myself and my purpose.*

*They're giving me more advice. "Be curious," they tell me. "Focus on your purpose and connect with us in the evening. Each day, write, reporting everything that is to do with the right purpose. When you practice this, you can stay focused, even when things appear not to be right. Now you can experience life in a positive and curious way. It is an adventure, one that you can appreciate. It doesn't matter if you are okay or not. It is not about wanting things. It is about looking and appreciating everything. It is also about appreciating what others have and being pleased for them."*

After her session, Mila struggles for some time, integrating this new way of being and staying out of the "soup."

Years later, I visit her in the cute cottage she managed to purchase. She lives close to the sea with her two precious dogs, who eventually came back to her. She walks them daily on the beach, loving the water and the beautiful sunsets. She has found some work and has many friends. She is full of joy and gratitude and loving her life.

Mila is learning that you cannot really love others unless your cup is full with love for yourself. Some might call it selfish, but in reality, we all need to balance service to ourselves with service to others.

## Sacrifice and Split Loyalties

Acting from love is not easy, especially when we are confronted with a choice between forsaking ourselves or forsaking others. What shall we do? Do we follow our own moral guidance and let others down, or do we submit to the needs of our loved ones? Ultimately, we have to live with the choices we make. As we survive physical death, living with the choices we make may mean sacrificing our physical life in order to be at peace with ourselves. Fortunately, most of us do not have to face such mortal decisions during our lives, but the next client, Trudy, did face this dilemma in a past life.

Trudy had a deep distrust for people apart from her own family. She came for a regression because she could find no reason in her current life for such strong feelings.

In the past life, she is Tatia, a young German nurse from Dusseldorf working near the front in WWII. Close by the German military camp is a ghetto where the Jewish people are being deliberately starved. Tatia is confronted with a terrible dilemma, for her father is the commander of the German brigade. Whatever she chooses will bring heartache or worse, for herself and for others.

Against strict orders, Tatia smuggles food to some of the besieged Jewish people. One day, she is dragged before her father. Her smuggling has been discovered.

*He is shouting in my face. My hands are tied in front of me and my hair is messy. Some others are lined up with me who have done something wrong. I cannot read my father's face, but I trust him to save me.*

*He is yelling at me, "Traitor, enemy, spy." Rations have been missing for a while, and he is telling everyone I am starving our soldiers. He had high expectations of me, and he is disappointed. He got me this job. He trusted me, and I let him down. I am a midwife, and I was recruited as an army nurse. It was supposed to be a privilege and opportunity, but it didn't feel like that to me. I feel awful, but I am angry with him and the soldiers. I don't think we should be doing this to the civilians. I am talking back to him, saying they are dying and starving and have done nothing wrong. He slaps me.*

*The people are Jewish. In my mind, they have done nothing wrong, but my father and the rest believe they are filth and cockroaches. That is what they are saying. I don't want to be a part of it. I don't regret what I have done.*

*Recently, I told my fiancé what I was doing. He is here too, a German soldier. He wasn't happy, but he didn't stop me. We have known each other a long time, since we were kids.*

*He and my father are very close. I trusted him, and he gave me up. I never expected him to do that. I think he needs my father's approval* more than mine. He doesn't agree with what I did. He is angry with me. He thinks I am a traitor too.

I want my father to trust me. I can see he has already made up his mind and turns away disgusted. I want him to be the loving father he was before. He was so nice when I was little, but I don't see that in him anymore. He doesn't care that I am his daughter. This means I am a war criminal. I thought he might save me and give me a lighter sentence.

The sentence is death. I cannot get past my father walking away. I turn to look at my promised husband, but he turns away too.

I was shot in the forehead. All my friends too. [Crying.]

I am upset about the other German people in the camp who died because of me. They had families. It was my fault. I didn't think they did anything wrong. I knew I wasn't supposed to do that, but I didn't care. I don't care that I did it. I convinced them to do it. I feel responsible for their deaths. I thought it would be okay.

I feel especially bad about the baker. I am friends with the baker's wife. I said sorry. He loves me like a daughter. He'd do anything for me. He is okay with dying. He didn't like what was happening either.

I suggest Tatia see her actions from the perspective of her father and fiancé.

They hated the Jews. We had been friends with some in the past. Now they saw them as trash, as vermin and cockroaches.

The war has been dragging on, and there are food shortages. They feel I betrayed them. My father cannot make an exception for me. He has to let me die. He is angry for me putting him in that position. He is angry with himself for bringing me there. I am an only child, and my mother has passed. I have put him in a terrible position. I am so stubborn.

Lissa is Jewish. I gave her children food. She was shot. I think it was my fault. She is smiling, saying I saved her. She was happy. I eased her *worry. Her children are okay. I helped keep them alive. She trusted me and loved me. She knows now that Germans are not all bad. I helped her feel human. I don't regret it.*

*My fiancé had no choice. He intended to turn me in privately to my father and stop it there, but I was seen by a German soldier handing over the food. He didn't want that. Once it was public, I couldn't be saved.*

*The guide said this life was about becoming stronger, trusting myself more and also learning to accept that sometimes we cannot fix everything or save everyone. I am not responsible for their happiness or their path.*

*I am sad that people have to suffer. I am being told that we have to cycle through many lessons and each time we do, we strengthen something in our soul. And sometimes we have to suffer to do that. It is an important lesson.*

*I came from love. I have had thousands of lives on planet earth. Sometimes I have been a bystander who did nothing. All they are saying is that I am becoming more open to love each lifetime, and I can be happy about that. I haven't done anything wrong; I am just growing.*

In the past life, Tatia tried to save others and it cost her life. She doesn't regret her decision. She couldn't stand by and watch people die. She sensed she had done that in earlier past lives. But at the time of the regression, she retained a kind of tunnel vision on what had happened, feeling hurt and disappointed with her father and her fiancé. Once she took a larger perspective, her hurt subsided and she could accept the actions of those she loved while still being at peace with her fatal decision.

Sometimes we have to act, even when the price is our life. Otherwise, we betray our true self and our compassion. It takes a strong soul to risk her life for another, but ultimately, we are all one. When we save another, we are saving ourselves too.

Tatia's other lesson was acceptance. Sometimes we are called to accept what we abhor, but we want to interfere because we cannot see the larger plan. Balancing our need to rebel with its opposite, our need to accept, can be tricky. We need wisdom and a greater perspective to find this balance.

## Conclusion

Rachel, Mila, and Trudy have undertaken soul journeys that shook them to the core. Consumed with feelings of worthlessness and anger, they might have spent countless lifetimes wandering in the dark. But when they were offered the chance to reconnect with joy, purpose, and love, they seized the opportunity.

We can still get lost on our way back to connection, but this is not what we want. Our guides are tasked with supporting us so we can recover quickly and not stay lost. In the lives explored in this chapter, each person faced conflictual situations they didn't want. Instead of resentment and bitterness, they made the best of the circumstances they faced.

In her past life, Rachel, as Tani, received help from the elders and members of the community. Like spiritual guides, they were kind and accepting, helping her soul learn to appreciate the value of mature love. When Mila asked for help, she received love, support, and encouragement from her guides and was able to embrace both her anger and her self-love.

Coming to an acceptance of ambiguity is one of the most profound spiritual lessons. Trudy, as Tatia, found herself being pulled in two directions between her sense of humanity and her loyalty to her family. She made a decisive choice, refusing to stand by and watch as people were mistreated. After her regression, she reconciled the choices her father and fiancé had made with her need to help the starving Jews. While she stood by her decision, she understood the bind she had created for both her father and fiancé. This realization gives Trudy a sense of inclusion and wholeness rather than division.

We are all tested on the road back to wholeness, which is really holiness. Being able to accept seemingly contradictory aspects of our personality is an essential step in our journey back to Source.

# SECTION 4:
# BUILDING BALANCE

# CHAPTER 10
# AVOIDING THE DEPTHS

At a high level, we are all one. Easy to say, but not so easy to accept. If we are all one, we would see the humanity in those who are cruel, callous, and heartless just as we do with those who are caring, loving, and compassionate. This is the goal of our journey.

We want to understand both victim and villain and the interplay between the two. Having taken these twin paths of separation and integrated our experiences, we intuitively know how both villain and victim suffer when disconnected from Source. Now, we can move from hate to acceptance, from judgment into compassion. This wisdom takes us to a place of peace.

This peace comes with a caveat, however. We cannot experience it unless we embrace ambiguity. This means accepting the whole rather than just those fragments of the whole that match our prejudices. It's easy for us to recognize the suffering of victims of abuse and hatred. It's much harder for us to acknowledge the humanity of the perpetrators. When perpetrators act out of their own pain, they create suffering for others and more pain for themselves in the future. Feeling compassion and love for all our brothers and sisters, victims and perpetrators alike, is only possible when we accept our shared humanity.

Those who remain estranged from Source cannot embrace this ambiguity. Victims who remain trapped in their victimhood are also disconnected from Source. For victims, as for perpetrators, ambiguity is the exact opposite of peace.

Some souls find it easier to embrace ambiguity than others. These souls are able to avoid taking a path of perpetration if that is what they choose. They have a strong sense of connection that is not easily broken. At pivotal moments of choice, they are likely to choose to trust and listen to guidance instead of taking willful actions of cynicism and anger.

Usually, these souls have had experiences on other planets and dimensions and retain a sense of their nonphysical nature. Still, they want to experience the separation from Source that earth offers. How can this be done?

These are trusting souls. They still have their share of anger and suffering. To experience separation, their natural innocence has to be disrupted as well as their connection to Source.

Because these are sensitive souls, their experiences of victimhood are different to many others. Their innate level of trust gives them a positive stance toward the challenges they will inevitably face on earth. Even when they do separate to some degree, feeling the negative emotions of hate and anger, their innate trust and positivity has them seeking answers. Their spiritual guidance returns, and before long they find forgiveness, compassion, and peace.

In this chapter, we meet some of these souls who avoid the heavy path of extreme separation. In Jasmine's case, we learn what it takes to disrupt one soul's connection to Source. Then Gisela shows us how one soul can forgive another, even though the second soul has been abusive in at least two of their shared incarnations. As naïve souls, Abigail and Melody experience some shocks when they incarnate within the earth system. Finally, Zelma reveals how even a bitter betrayal can provide rich learnings for a soul.

# Disrupting a Strong Source Connection

Jasmine, a young woman in her twenties, came to see me a couple of years after her father died. She felt a wave of tremendous grief at his loss and was still upset. Loss is one of the rich experiences earth offers, and transcending loss presents another challenge for souls to overcome. While Jasmine processed the loss of her father during her regressions, another significant insight emerged. During her previous sixty-two earth incarnations, Jasmine had never experienced anger.

This seems surprising when you consider some of her past lives. In 1536, she watched her friend burn at the stake. Jasmine felt sad, but this incident did not provoke her anger. In another life, she was ignored by her fellow villagers because she couldn't communicate. She was not concerned, because she spent her short life in the forest connected with nature.

In her most recent past life as Felicja, she experienced heart-rending tragedy. She lived with her family in Eastern Poland until the Soviets annexed her home region in 1939.

Jealous neighbors reported her family to the authorities. While Felicja was busy in town one day, the Soviets came and arrested her entire family. She went looking for them, but it was too late—they had already been killed. The soldiers threw her into prison. Although devastated by the loss of her family, Felicja didn't feel anger. The prison guards sexually assaulted her before they shot her. Despite this brutal treatment, she retained her connection to Source energy, focusing on positivity, compassion, and beauty. After dying, she weeps while explaining how she feels.

*I am floating above. Everything is so beautiful. I can see the buildings and it is a beautiful place, a small town. The buildings are wooden and have been there for a long time. The only ugly one is the place where I was held and died. It is made of concrete bricks, unpainted, purpose-built, and ugly.*

One of the soldiers who was forced to shoot her is upset. He cared for her and didn't want her to die. She drifts back to the courtyard of the prison where she finds him slumped against the wall.

*I am worried about the guy who shot me. He is crying. I am trying to get through to him, but he can't hear me. I have my hand on his shoulder, and he is sobbing.*

Her innate compassion was stronger than any other emotion and even as she ascended, her focus was on beauty not what she'd suffered.

Later, during her life between lives regression, we discover she is on her last earth incarnation—not because she is fully enlightened, but because the earth system is too dense for her sensitive nature. Her guides tell her there are other, gentler places where she can incarnate.

Jasmine tells her guides she wants to leave before suffering any more loss. They chuckle, then confess that they were surprised she chose to incarnate on earth in the first place. They knew her delicate nature could not withstand the human instinct for violence. As her soul-self, she speaks briefly about a few of her early incarnations.

*I have been on a long journey, and I have come back to myself. I had one very early life on earth when people were just starting to be civilized. I didn't come back to earth for a long time after that. I didn't incarnate on other planets. I waited—waited until humans developed.*

Before she came to her present and final incarnation, her guides suggested she take advantage of the density of earth to experience the anger she had missed. Jasmine had no understanding of the emotions of hate and anger. Although she had observed these emotions in others, she had never felt them herself. In this life, she agreed to experience anger.

When she was a teen, she was brutalized and sexually assaulted by a psychopath. She felt angry and lots of other emotions too. Her father was there for her and helped her cope. But the abuse wasn't the end of her suffering. Even though he knew what she had endured, the prosecutor in her legal case spent six hours harassing her to sign a document denying the allegation of sexual assault and declaring that the sex had been consensual.

*As a soul, I wanted to see how much I could cope with. My guides warned me, telling me I was biting off more than I could chew. I am proud of my ability to cope with things, and I wanted to show off. I had never had a life where I was angry, and I needed to experience rage, anger, frustration, and wanting to tear myself apart. I have only gotten past that anger in the last few years, and it was difficult.*

*I was angry at everyone around me. My guides are saying that was part of the plan and there is no need to feel guilty for my reactions. I was trying to find out what it was like to have that angry energy. We planned to have people be cruel and mean to me, doctors and people at school. I wondered why they treated me like that. Now, I am being shown that each one agreed to play that role.*

*A lot of them are still in that angry space at this time. They are fiery souls and it is easy for them to play those roles at this point in their development. It is part of their nature right now. The ones who hurt me the most deliberately took on that energy to play those roles. The abuser has done things like that in the past, and he is repeating the same behavior over and over. I haven't known him in other lives. As a soul, he wants to get past it, but once he arrives down here on the planet, he gets trapped in the same pattern. Many get trapped in their patterns.*

*The other one is the prosecutor of the legal case that went on for years. He knew I couldn't get through a trial. He tore me to shreds, yelling at me for six hours, wanting me to say I was a willing participant. I eventually gave in. The prosecutor benefited from my mental breakdown afterward. He couldn't stop thinking about it, regretting the way he treated me. He changed and gave up being a prosecutor.*

*The abuser got a one-year sentence, but I don't know how much he served. I know he is part of a pedophile ring. They wanted him to turn others in, so that is why the prosecutor wanted me to sign. It was expedient, but it broke me.*

*I didn't have much compassion for angry people until I had this experience. My guides are pretty happy that I decided to go for it and have this challenging life.*

Jasmine has been strongly connected to her larger self during her lives on earth. It took extreme abuse to interrupt this connection, allowing her to feel the human emotions of anger and hate. To us, such suffering is deplorable, and many would find it hard to forgive the abuser. Not Jasmine, however. She forgave him in order to free herself. Naturally, she wanted him to be punished in accordance with the law. That is why the prosecutor's behavior was so devastating to her.

Jasmine's current perspective on her experience is very different to that of most people. Yes, she was angry at first. As her guides explained, there is nothing wrong with being outraged and angry. That is a valid reaction to sexual abuse. But Jasmine eventually took a larger perspective, helping her understand the challenges she faced over many lifetimes. She now knows why humans sometimes feel like killing and hurting people, although she never acted on her anger. Jasmine didn't need to go down the perpetrator path. She knows exactly why she chose these difficult lives and what she learned from them. For her, that has been useful. Five years after her session, she said she is happy and doing well in life.

## Betrayed but Unbroken

Self-doubt is debilitating and being the victim of violence is awful. At a soul level, however, these experiences can be illuminating, especially when souls retain a strong Source connection that stops them falling into the painful path of serious separation. Our next case tells the story of one such soul.

Gisela is a businesswoman with a coaching and mediation business. During her regression, I ask her if she has been a perpetrator in any of her lives.

*I haven't needed to go down the dark path. I have felt frustrated and angry with my ex-husband and thought about harming him, but I caught myself. I couldn't follow through with it. That higher power, that sense of self, tells me it is not right to do that.*

*I have always known of some higher, powerful energy. I don't intentionally do any wrong to another. I haven't felt any need for revenge. Instead, I would run and hide. I have had lives where I've been killed.*

*I have been down a different path, one where I serve others and sacrifice myself. I am still learning how to balance serving myself and serving others.*

Even in her current life, Gisela has suffered. Her first husband died of cancer when she was young. She soon met a man called Wolfgang whom she described as amazing. She was happy for a dozen years until his behavior started to change. One day, she picked him up from the airport and sensed something was wrong.

*He didn't kiss me. A voice said, "Look in that backpack." I thought it was unethical, but I looked. He was actually living a double life. I had him followed and investigated. He was having an affair in another city and stealing money from my business. I discovered he had $100,000*

189

*worth of debt that I didn't know about. He didn't even have a driver's license, although he drove. There were so many lies.*

*Most people saw our relationship as happy and the two of us as a great team. A few sensed something dubious about him, but no one said anything because I was so happy. He was always extremely sweet and smooth, never missing a beat, always having an answer.*

After they parted, Gisela couldn't quite understand how she had been duped for so long. She came for a regression to find out.

In a past life, she is Constance, the illegitimate daughter of a noble, while her mother is a servant who works in the castle. Constance senses a private kindness in her father's manner toward her. We go to a scene when Constance is in her late twenties.

*Oh my gosh! The castle is mine. My father passed away and left it to me and my mother. His other children were perplexed. He gave them some story and made it watertight. They left. I think he loved me. I was a happy, positive child, and he recognized that I was his. We had a connection in spite of him being distant. It all changed after he died.*

*I am married. My husband wooed me, and I fell under his spell. Once we were married, he changed. Now he is quiet, sullen, and disinterested in me. I see him sitting beside me and his energy has no color, no vibrancy. He's like a vampire, sucking energy from others. When I am happy and positive, he drinks. When I am emotionally and physically depleted, he feels strong. And when I am strong, he feels weak.*

I move Constance along into another scene of her life, but she is in darkness. When I ask what happened, she replies sparsely in a small, sad voice.

*I am floating in darkness in space. Death. I was trapped and smothered in the castle . . . in the dungeon. It was the husband. [Crying.] He planned it . . . and targeted me because of my inheritance.*

*I just accepted what happened because, deep down, I didn't feel worthy. It's almost like I was waiting for it to be taken away. It didn't feel right in the first place, as I was illegitimate and from lowly circumstances. I didn't earn it. My father just gave it to me out of guilt and love.*

*I can see my body in the dungeon. I am outside. I went straight up. I knew to leave the body there. I am with my paternal grandfather [in my current life]. There is so much love. [Crying.] He was a hard man but beautiful to me. His soul is the same as the father who left me the castle.*

I ask about the importance of Constance's life.

*I am not to change. I am to stay true to who I really am, positive and happy. I get a sense that I was congruent, true, and authentic. I was just gullible. My guide is putting his hand on my head saying that I was a good soul. I trusted, taking that person at face value. I did get some hints that the husband wasn't authentic but, coming from an impoverished background, I didn't trust my own judgment. I didn't take notice of the hints.*

Gisela experiences two other past lives. One is in Paris with a husband she loves deeply before dying young in 1920. Soon after, she reincarnates in Italy, where she is widowed in her early thirties. Her love for her husband lives on, and her two sons work their successful farm. I ask about the purpose of these two lives.

*These are my "go to" for the rest of this current life. In the Parisian and Italian lives, I was grounded and connected to Source with a sense of knowing. My guide smiles and places his hand on my head. He is saying I already know what I need to know but I don't trust it. I get caught up in self-doubt. Other people read me incorrectly, thinking I am strong and arrogant. They like to bring my all-knowing energy down.*

*I asked if there was anything I can do to stop people treating me this way. He said, "No." It is a test, a reminder to stay authentic no matter what others do. I am standing, and he is floating above me. There is more than one. He is the leader.*

I ask about her experience with Wolfgang and his duplicity.

*I need to stay authentic and strong because there was a reason for it. I have been part of a plan, and I can get on now with the rest of my life. I have to forgive myself for thinking I didn't make the right judgment call. I feel confused. What Wolfgang did I can see as a rejection, or I can see it as a gift to him because I am a loving person.*

*Wolfgang is not open and curious enough to realize what he has done in this life. I can forget about him saying sorry. There is no sense of an end at this stage. It was Wolfgang who smothered me in that past life. He had no feeling about it, no sorrow at all. He has been going down that dark path. He doesn't know how to feel. He is numb. He cut his feelings off because it is the only way he knows how to get what he needs.*

*Now I see him [in one of his past lives] as a child in a tunnel, living underground with nothing, not even a parent. He is in England, very poor. He became bitter, wanting to get even with those who have material possessions when he has nothing. The karma is carried over from lifetime to lifetime until you get out of it.*

Gisela is able to feel compassion for Wolfgang, even though she hasn't been down the perpetrator path. She understands how lost he is. No bitterness remains for the way he behaved toward her. I ask Gisela about her soul journey through her lifetimes.

*I have had lives on other planets. I haven't had many lives on earth. I came from light. I had a lot of experience on other planets, and I had learned a lot already.*

*I am ethical, and yet it doesn't feel right; my ethics seem to be contaminated in some way, out of kilter. I am asking my guide why that is. He says because I try to do the right thing all the time. I offer information and then doubt what I said. I just need to be aware of this tendency to self-doubt.*

*I am part of those who are here to serve. The leader is someone within the group. We are always connected with each other and on the same vibration.*

Obviously, Gisela didn't need to go down a dark path. Even though she can fall into self-doubt, she has gained much experience, knowledge, and wisdom. As a sensitive, light soul, her spirit guides respect her vulnerability and only give her what she can manage. She is learning to remain authentic to herself no matter how much dishonesty, betrayal, and loss she encounters.

Gisela feels naïve, but her guide congratulates her for taking her corrupt husband at face value. Her naïve trust was part of the plan—her love and trust a gift for his lost soul.

A couple of years later, I speak to her. She has met a kind man who shares the same soul as her beloved Paris husband. When they met, they connected immediately and now share an unbreakable bond. She is joyous once again.

## Victimized Yet Victorious

Like Gisela, Abigail has lived on other planets in previous lives. During her regression, Abigail's guides give her information about the path she has taken through the earth system.

*I came in on a less traumatic path. I have been given what I could handle. I did have lives of suffering and hardness. I have been to hell while incarnated. I see myself in a dungeon in a past life. I was a normal male in France but became caught up in this war, rounded up, and thrown into the dungeon. Chained to the wall and sitting on a dirty, cold, stone floor, I am ugly and skinny with a beard down to my torso. That is hell. I died in that dungeon in 1628. I went back to my cabin in the afterlife for seventeen years.*

*I haven't been violent in past lives. The guides are saying, "You didn't want to go down that rough path. You came from a different universe. You have been on other planets, which were peaceful and worthwhile, with much creativity. In many lifetimes, you were part of a collective, like cogs in a wheel that helped everything go around. In that system, all were equal."*

*But I wanted to experience an earth life: the independence, the variety, the emotions. I came in balanced while earth isn't. I am here to grow and to learn how to be calm and peaceful while on earth. Worry is fear. I am here to conquer fear and enjoy myself. Earth is full of wonderful things.*

Abigail's higher soul-self decided to experience life on planet earth. Even though she has been thrown out of balance during her journey, guidance from her experienced higher self helps get her back on track.

Souls such as Jasmine, Gisela, and Abigail have tended to be innocent and trusting in some of their lives. Melody, our next case, also sees herself as naïve.

## Melody: Seeing Truth

In her regressions, Melody experiences a number of lives. In one, she is murdered by people jealous of her healing powers. In another, she is selfish, although she has no intention of hurting anyone. She just values her freedom and having her own way. In a third, she is bitter and beastly, like a feral animal, scratching and attacking people. She is jailed, sexually assaulted, and beaten until she eventually submits. Then she turns 180 degrees, helping heal sick and distressed women in the prison. In one life, much earlier in the earth's history, she is a pagan who lives in nature and is invested with magical powers.

During Melody's session, I ask why she is so naïve in this life.

*I come from a different plane of existence where it is all transparent, open, and honest. And I don't want to believe that people can be vicious.*

*I am asking to be able to see the truth of all people. I need to see them as they are.*

*Now I am more relaxed. It is good to see the truth. I can see that the walls I put up are about my lack of discrimination. I don't need the great big wall. Instead, I can be compassionate and choose to not be around aggressive, ignorant people. In the palm of my hand, I am given a piece of clear quartz. "That is the clarity," the guides say.*

*They are doing something to my ears. It is helping me hear what people really say. It is about knowing what people are saying beneath what they say. A lot of people say things but what they say is loaded. They have a double meaning that I have not picked up. I have been walking through this world blind and deaf, very innocent. Now I am walking through the world with wisdom from my intuition.*

During her session, Melody makes many connections to her current life and between her lives, gaining a deep understanding of human nature through all her experiences. Although she has been unhappy about her naivety, there is power in naïve trust, as we will discover in our next case.

## Learning Through Trust

Zelma comes to a life between lives regression feeling alone since the breakup of her fifteen-year relationship with Manfred. After the marriage ends, she continues to reside in the same house with Manfred, mainly for financial reasons. The relationship is now platonic, but Zelma still hopes their love might be rekindled.

One day, after a couple of years living together as housemates, Zelma and Manfred discuss who will look after the cat during a long weekend. Manfred reluctantly admits he plans to travel across the country to be with his friend Clare and her family. He was close to Clare even before he married Zelma, but he always described the relationship as platonic. Until this discussion, Zelma saw nothing that convinced her otherwise, but now the penny drops. Zelma shouts at him, "You are in a relationship with her!" Manfred finally admits the truth. He and Clare have been in a romantic relationship for years. Zelma is devastated by his betrayal.

When Zelma comes to the regression, she thinks she is over Manfred. She wants to find another partner because she is tired of being alone and, in her own words, "invisible to men."

During the regression, Zelma accesses a life as a German soldier in World War II.

The solider is assigned to one of the concentration camps where he supervises people being herded into the gas chambers. A trusting soul, he puts his doubts aside, accepting the Nazi propaganda that Jewish people are subhuman and need to be eliminated.

One day, he observes a young teenage boy patiently and lovingly assist his invalid father into the showers—actually, the gas chambers. The soldier is shaken. How can such kindness be the action of subhumans?

The scales fall from his eyes. He realizes the state has been lying to him all these years. Soon, he is talking about it to his fellow soldiers, unsettling them and causing problems for the commandant. He is asked to retract his views but refuses, so he is shot as a traitor.

When she was younger, Zelma remembers stumbling into a place in Hungary where she couldn't stop crying. She was confused, not knowing why she was so upset. Even when she discovered the place was a Holocaust memorial, she didn't fully understand why it touched her so deeply.

I ask if she can see any similarities between the betrayal in the past life by the Nazis and the betrayal by Manfred. Zelma looks thoughtful before exclaiming.

*They lied to me! I trusted them, and they all lied to me!*

She is silent for a long time, and something deeply shifts within her. A month after the regression, Zelma writes to me.

*I was talking to a friend today, and I said, "From the heart, I wish my ex-husband well and I hope he is happy with his partner, Clare." I didn't realize until I said that how much distress I have felt for so many years about his deceit. Now I feel truly free.*

Zelma was deeply hurt by the Nazis' lies in the past life and by Manfred's lies during their relationship. She suffered hurt and anger for fifteen years with Manfred before she'd had enough. She was angry with herself, angry with her naivety. She'd had a few moments of doubt, but she couldn't see through the deception.

The German soldier had trusted untrustworthy people, and Zelma had done the same in her current life. It took time before the soldier and Zelma had the wisdom to clearly see through the lies and get back in touch with their true selves.

Ultimately, nothing was lost. Zelma's soul gained. By suffering these betrayals and taking time later to reflect, understand, and integrate her experiences, she enhanced her wisdom. Integrated experience develops our soul's wisdom and forms the basis of our intuition. Anyone trying to deceive her in future will find it much more difficult. She will be listening and acting on her intuition.

## Conclusion

Trust can be a shortcut through the earth system. Specifically, this means trusting that whatever happens in life is occurring for a good reason. It is not easy to stay trusting, and it is natural for humans to have doubts. Each of the people in this chapter had times when they doubted their path. However, they all managed to re-establish their trust in Source relatively quickly.

Perpetrators lack trust in a higher power. They cut themselves off from Source. We can avoid the perpetrator path when we maintain that strong upward connection, trusting that all that happens is purposeful. This doesn't mean we avoid challenging lives of suffering. But it does mean the challenges we face are meaningful. They are opportunities to learn. Souls who retain a connection to Source, hearing guidance and acting upon it, will learn quickly.

Can we miss the lesson? Yes, but not forever. Lack of trust is the path of blame, anger, and bitterness. In other words, victimhood, which means looking outside of ourselves for the cause of our distress. Eventually, we learn to look inside. If we ask for insight with a genuine desire to see the truth, we will have experiences that draw our attention to our faulty beliefs, behavior, and history. This is what happens in the regressions. Relevant scenarios are relived and connections are made. Clients are given the opportunity to see the truth and integrate it into their current lives.

The souls in this chapter have a strong connection to Source. They sense that nothing can ultimately hurt them even when, as humans living on a difficult planet, they have periods of doubt. Their souls have been imprinted with the wisdom that all will be well, while souls taking a perpetrator path are more deeply imprinted with fear.

# CHAPTER 11
# INNER STRENGTH AND BALANCE

When we look at the yin and yang symbol, we see it is in perfect balance, being made up of two opposing parts of a unified whole. The two halves represent seemingly opposing forces—light and dark, masculine and feminine, sun and moon—which actually complement and depend upon each other. If one half grows larger, it throws the whole out of balance.

Apparently, two dots indicate that there is always yin within yang, and yang within yin, but I also interpret it as flexibility. When expressing one side, we are aware of the other. We need to know weakness to recognize strength, and we need to experience strength to understand weakness. Then we learn to refine these two extremes so we can express whatever is needed in any given situation. This is how we maintain our equilibrium.

Balance is not just a measure of our spiritual development; it is vitally important in all aspects of our lives.

## How We Maintain Balance

Our physical bodies are always striving for balance. The alkaline–acid balance in our blood is precise and has to be preserved to sustain life. To maintain this ratio, our kidneys will rob our bones of calcium if necessary. Our glucagon and insulin balance also needs to be maintained, as any diabetic can tell you. Our pancreas instructs the liver to give up its glucagon stores to stop us going into a coma when our blood sugar drops too low. We can die very quickly if the blood sugar is not restored.

Balance will be maintained while we live. But what price must we pay to maintain balance? If our blood is consistently acidic, we can develop osteoporosis. If our heart struggles to pump enough blood to the cells, it may enlarge. The same question is relevant when considering our emotional and psychological health.

In previous chapters, you met a number of past life characters who were perpetrators, predators, and victims. While caught in these desolate lives, none of them exhibited healthy levels of emotional or psychological balance. Unable to maintain the proper balance, they found another way to survive. Their compulsive, dysfunctional behavior enabled them to function and keep going. The vampiric mercenary we met in chapter 5 couldn't survive without the woman he misused. After her suicide, he went back to war to die in battle. He fed the emptiness within by taking the lives of his enemies, by robbing them of their psychic energy. This allowed him to function.

In contrast to the mercenary, who was always out of kilter, the yin-yang symbol represents healthy balance. We seek this balance through experience, gained through multiple incarnations. One client, Edward, is shown how this works during his regression.

*The guide is taking me to another lifetime where I have been wealthy and part of the nobility. It feels like I am being frivolous, careless, condescending to others, and wasteful toward people. I feel above the poor. Here I am irresponsible. It is a life in Persia with very pretty marble floors, rich furnishings, and lots of women. I am a male who is very self-indulgent. Now we are going somewhere else.*

*I am in London, or somewhere like it, where it is chilly and wet, with a grey sky and bleak stone buildings. I am poor, homeless, cold, and hungry. I have lived both ends of the extreme. There is a second guide who is reaching out his hands in both directions, indicating each extreme at opposite ends of the continuum. Both guides are saying it is about getting balance. In the middle lie responsibility, balance, and conscious thought processes about the appropriate use of resources.*

Finding balance cannot be easily achieved if we avoid experiencing the extremes. Most souls choose to experience each end of a continuum, whether it be war and peace, connection and separation, or strength and vulnerability.

We do not develop balance by taking resources away. Balance requires addition. As we develop the strength and courage required to defend ourselves, we are also given opportunities to learn generosity and humility. We develop the ability to access opposing qualities as well as all configurations in between the two extremes.

## Out of Balance

As we have seen, being out of balance physically means illness or death. Psychological imbalance can also be fatal.

One young client, Máté, had a friend who committed suicide. People who commit suicide tend to be out of balance and unable to maintain even an unhealthy balance. During his regression,

Máté is curious about his friend and receives reassurance from his guides.

> *Your friend is fine. Losing connection is something that everyone experiences to varying degrees.*

It is never really planned for any soul to choose to leave their body this way, but when it happens, those who remain have an opportunity to learn. They are affected, and it becomes important for them. Nothing is wasted.

Suicide is a fork down the path that, when chosen, truncates the soul's previous path. But it opens up opportunities for others. Life plans are well thought out and organized, but always in motion. The plan is as alive as the souls themselves. Everyone has a choice. To be in constant flux is the nature of everything. Energy itself is in flux and is there to indicate a course, a direction. Suicide is not a prominent path for anyone. While it does help others, anyone who commits suicide will eventually have to overcome a forfeit of love for the soul.

Disconnection is a path that all souls in the earth system need to experience, but not necessarily to the same degree. Suicide is a rejection of life, of being, of others, and of connection to Source. Souls use their free will to choose leaving a life prematurely.

## Developing Healthy Balance

Souls can evolve without having traumatic lives, but there is a richness missing. Those souls that choose to take the deeper path into the dark night of the soul can eventually develop a profound appreciation for life. The deeper the experience of darkness, including hatred, emptiness, loneliness, and despair, the deeper the appreciation of connection, joyfulness, and love.

We develop healthy balance through experience. We experience both extremes of the continuum and then work at finely tuning our sense of all the qualities involved. We are seeking wholeness and perfection, hoping we will always make great decisions. But nothing in the world of duality lasts. Everything is dynamic. In one regression, we are told how balance is a worthwhile attainment but cannot be preserved:

*In a way, balance is like juggling jelly. It is good, but it takes a lot of work. Flow is the natural state. Order does not last. Everything flows, spiraling from disorder to order then back to disorder and so on. Nothing is still; life is always moving. Even after physical death, the flow continues.*

Because everything is in flux, describing someone as good or bad is greatly limited. It's not so easy to pin us down. We are all subject to constant change. We are always moving along the continuum of two extremes because the circumstances we face are also constantly changing. For example, all souls need to develop both strength and vulnerability, but they also need draw on all the subtleties that lie in between the two extremes. In doing so, they cultivate their inner strength. They hone the ability to be forceful and flexible, strong and vulnerable, tough and gentle, courageous and timid, confident and humble—not necessarily exercising both extremes in the same moment, but rather expressing whatever quality and intensity is appropriate in each particular circumstance.

The next case explores a past life where this balance between strength and vulnerability is being dynamically developed and tested.

## A Life of Inner Strength and Balance

Justin is a musician. Somewhere along the line, he has picked up the idea he is not smart. Lately, he feels stuck and unable to implement his ideas. His desire is to inspire people, but he fears that he lacks the strength needed to do so.

During his regression, he experiences a past life as Mushta, who lived on the coast of North Africa many years ago. As we will see, Mushta overcomes a series of trials, developing a resilient inner strength.

*I am like a child but no longer a child, like a man but not yet a man. I am a young teen. Standing on the edge of a sandy beach, I see the sun slowly sinking in the sky. My upper body is in sun while the rest is in shade. Beside me is a well and temporary dwellings made from skins and poles. These come with us when we travel, as we are a small group of nomads. While other members of our company bustle around preparing food and looking after our few donkeys and goats, I am carving a piece of wood, a task assigned to me by my father.*

*I pause. I sense danger. I watch my father.*

*He has a half-grey beard, wearing leather sandals, a white gown, and a cloth wrapped around his head. He is smart, always cautious, always one step ahead, always working to keep us safe.*

*The danger comes suddenly when I see a small army of men stirring up dust as they gallop toward us on fast horses. Dressed in white, these men wave curved swords in the air, their heads and faces wrapped in dark cloth, revealing nothing but black, flaring eyes.*

*They stop and dismount, rushing at us. I see they are callous, pushing people out of the way, demolishing our belongings, intimidating the women and children. In spite of witnessing flashes of violence, I am rooted to the same spot.*

*Suddenly, I feel a powerful hand on my thin arm. I recoil, but the thick hand tightens its grip, pulling at me as if am nothing. Cold eyes send me a message: "Killing you would be easy. This is just what we do. It's business. We don't want to kill you, but if you don't submit, we will." This man is dangerous. He backhands me savagely across the face. I know it is a warning to take him seriously and not risk messing with him. He smacks me around like a plaything, dragging me away while I cover my head with my hands in a vain attempt to protect myself.*

*I see my father on the ground with his arm bleeding. He looks up at me calmly, sending me a message to also stay calm. He knows how to survive and how to fight, but he is not fighting now. He is wise. He knows when to do what he is told.*

*The raiders surround us. They are taking things and people. They are taking me.*

*My father looks at me, saying with his eyes, "Surrender and go." My heart is pounding until I feel his calm, wise strength penetrate my thin, slight body. My mother is hiding, afraid and still.*

*The raiders wave their scimitars, yelling threats, wanting us to feel scared. They take our food, our grain, our goats, and our boys.*

*The dangerous man, the one who grabbed me, throws me like a bag of beans across the back of his horse. The other boys, younger than me, are all thrown across the horses in the same uncomfortable position, lying virtually in the lap of each rider, denying us any means of escape. The dangerous man barks at my father, warning him not to follow us, departing with the words, "We will be back."*

*I see my mother's face, her dismay, her disappointment. I know she has seen this before, perhaps when she was a girl of the same age as my little sister who is now hiding behind our mother's robe. I sense that she hoped she would never see it again.*

*Before the horses take off, the dangerous man drags me off the horse, positioning me upright, seated behind him. He knows I am not going to run away. He knows how afraid I am.*

*We are riding over sand hills and desert until, hours later, we come to a hilly place like a village—but not a village—more like an enclave of dwellings made of cloth and poles. I see lots of these battered and half buried, temporary abodes—a testament to the relentless assault of wind and sand and the length of time they have been in this place.*

*Giving me a look of stone, a warning of dire consequences if I try to escape, the dangerous man throws me off the horse. Other men carry the stolen food into a cave dug out of the hill. Someone behind us, a man who cares nothing for our welfare, shoves us savagely into this cave. The cave is dark, and it takes time for my eyes to adjust to the flickering light. Now I see filthy carpets with dirt and rubbish lying around carelessly.*

*The dangerous man is now beside me, and I see my future with him. I call him Master, but that is not the word, although that is what it means in English. These men steal boys to add to their numbers because raiders do not live long lives.*

*Master is like a soldier, and he teaches me to fight, hurting me, toughening me up to become a raider like him. At first, I am not good at learning because I am too soft and gentle. He is brutal, kicking me, punching me, leaving me in the desert overnight, cutting me in mock battle, until eventually my survival instinct kicks in and I turn hard and cold like him.*

*He teaches me how to kill. By the time I am trained, Master knows he is slowing down, his final fight looming before him. He has been brutal—starving me, beating me, and isolating me. Although his hardness leaves no room for affection, I know he enjoys bringing out the strength in me, seeing me prevail over the ordeals he sets for me, and watching me grow vicious and tough.*

*There were times when the other raiders wanted to kill me, thinking I was weak and worthless, but he protected me, saying, "I'll stand for him." And then he taught me how to protect myself.*

*My master is dead. He didn't die in battle like he wanted. He became ill, coughing up blood, refusing to let me hold his hand while dying, looking at me with his hard eyes, insisting on no pity.*

*I am still young, twenty-four, but I feel older. My complexion is dark from the sun and years of accumulated grime ground into my skin. My body is scarred, my face—the left side—permanently busted, always hurting, always throbbing. I feel dirty, constantly dirty. Sand is always in my eyes and, although I am used to the dirt and sand, I have never liked it. I am tired, really tired. I don't want to fight anymore. I liked my master's admiration and my skill at killing, but I don't really like ending people's lives.*

*They let me go. My master paid for me so that, after he died, I could be free. Did he see something in me when he first grabbed me as I baulked at his touch—something, perhaps, he saw in himself? Did he really want to enslave me? Now, I doubt it. He, too, was captured and forced to fight, then later he captured me and forced me to fight. I did the same, capturing a boy, throwing him on a horse, and carrying him away. But I didn't train him. I left.*

*I have seen my family from time to time, in the distance, but they never see me. One day in a market town, my headscarf loosened; my sister sees me and says my name. I hold her arms gently for a moment, smile, and leave.*

*I do not go to them.*

Mushta has survived. Taken from his family, he made the best of his situation, wisely submitting while learning how to be strong and protect himself. His patience has been rewarded with his freedom. Now, he is physically strong but weak in the order of possessions and any skills apart from fighting.

Going back to his family would be a backward step. Mushta knows that as a man he needs to make his own way in the world.

*I struggle through the desert on foot until I arrive in a market town, a place with beaches and sea nearby, buildings of mud and stone, dwellings of cloth and poles. I look like a raider—dangerous, hungry, and dirty. I am on the fringes, pegged as a criminal, trying to blend in but distrusted, avoided, and sometimes threatened.*

*For several months, I fish outside the town, just to eat. I finally take off my scarf, clean myself up, and grow a beard. I feel lost. [Crying.] I don't know who I am. I want peace.*

*I deliberately teach myself to walk like a normal person rather than a raider. I am dangerous, but I make myself look peaceful and swear to be a man of peace. I know my father now: his strength, his toughness, his wisdom, always alert for trouble, always planning to avoid the raiders, and I realize he had a life like this. I bury my scimitar in sand near some trees, hoping to never need it again.*

*I hang around the market until one day a grey-bearded man asks me to help him. Even though, from my scars, he suspects I have a past, he pays me to move his wares of jars, tools, utensils, carpets, barrels— all sorts of trading goods.*

*I am attracted to his daughter, her long-lashed eyes glancing at me from time to time, turning away shyly whenever I catch her eye.*

*Her father loans me money, letting me start my own small business while still working for him. I learn by watching while he watches me struggling to count properly, finding this particular clumsiness of mine endearing.*

*Eventually, I ask to marry his daughter, Anguilla, whose eyes constantly follow me. He agrees. I have to give him a dowry, and that will take years of work. People like me, and I do well. Knowing how to look after myself, I am at ease with myself, developing the charm I saw in my father. I am yearning to be married to Anguilla, so I work hard. Remembering the harsh life I have left behind, I am happy.*

*Never having spoken to each other, we marry, taking time to get to know each other. There is an intimacy that grows between us, a mutual trust. I love kissing her soft and delicate hands, begging her not to do harsh work, rushing to do her chores or instructing the servants to do them for her. She laughs and tells me she is not useless. I feel strong because of her love and inspired to do well.*

*After she becomes a mother, she grows into a strong woman. I knew nothing about women until I married Anguilla. Now I feel so safe with her, making love feels like coming home.*

A few years later, Mushta lives in a grand house on the hill looking over the ocean. He is well respected for his hard work and honesty. Now, he has children aged from three to seven.

*I am a trader of cloth, seeds, grains, and exotic fruits and vegetables. I import and export these wares on schooners that I see coming and going as I look down on the bay.*

*I have my wife, a beautiful woman who trusts me. I care for her deeply. The business does well, and I expand, encouraging the boat traders to bring in new exotic fruits and vegetables, including seedlings that Anguilla likes to coax into life.*

With his patience and persistence, Mushta has found the right balance between submission and control with his workers, customers, friends, and family. He is always respectful but can be soft or firm depending on what is needed. This approach has bought him success. We go to the end of his life.

*I die old—old for then—in my fifties, my beard not entirely grey, my son a man. Like my master, I die of a disease in the lungs, coughing up a lot of blood, in pain until the end. Anguilla is beside me, crying, wishing me peace, saying that I've been a good man.*

*I never told her what I did in the past, but she knew I'd had a violent life. She would kiss my scars.*

*I pass slowly, pain gnawing into my chest and stomach. I die, climbing out of myself. Anguilla cries, cleaning the blood from my mouth, kissing my mouth and cheek. Now my son is holding her. I reach out to let them know that all is well.*

*I trust she will be fine, having done a deal with a trusted friend to look after her. I taught my boy to be tough—not in the way I was taught, not harshly, but sufficiently for him to look after his mother. Men want her and the business and wealth. I gave the business to my son, telling him to grow his beard so he looks more mature.*

*I watch her through the years, sitting with her at times, sensing her pleasant memories of us together, seeing her with our grandchildren. I see her growing older and still beautiful with her amazing skin and shock of grey hair. She lives in the same place, and sometimes she feels lonely for me.* [Cries.]

*I can still feel her love, such a powerful love. She gave me a chance to redeem myself, sensing my need for redemption without knowing the details.*

Mushta's life is an important learning for Justin, who lost his way on his soul journey.

*In my current life, I have always harbored a fear of feeling weak. I have spent all my life trying to be strong—not acting strong but wanting to genuinely feel strong, knowing I show my vulnerability too much.*

Justin finds out how he came to be out of balance.

*After Mushta, I believed that if I am strong, I must be brutal. So I chose softer lives but became weak. Now I need to find my way back.* [Cries.] *In my current life, I was born with weak joints on purpose. When I was sixteen, a doctor said my knees were weak and my shoulders were underdeveloped.*

Justin is afraid of his own strength. He recalls how Mushta was better balanced.

*I remember young Mushta being tough, and my journey is to learn to be both strong and compassionate. As an older man, Mushta incorporated the strength he learned as a raider to be able to live calmly, without fear, among others, including tough businessmen. He had the inner strength and the softness, expressing both well.*

Mushta was skilled and tough when in battle as a raider. He was strong and friendly as a businessman. And he was soft, vulnerable, and loving as a husband and father. This is an expression of balance. He had many abilities and qualities, ranging from one extreme to the other, and he was wise in choosing when to use each one.

## Conclusion

Developing inner strength and balance is a crucial part of our journey as we move closer to its end. Inner strength is the opposite of self-doubt. It means having faith in ourselves and our abilities. We trust that we are lovable, loved, and protected, sensing a connection to Source, with no need to make any proclamation of its power. We don't need to be defensive or offensive, accepting others where they are. We have strong boundaries, setting them gently and sincerely so others soon know what we stand for. We appreciate connection and beauty and enjoy seeing others do well. We are grateful for what we have and make the best of our resources and talents, taking advantage of opportunities to learn and do better. Mushta's life exemplifies these qualities. While not easy in the beginning, it was a life well lived.

Whatever we experience in life is useful. So many of us judge ourselves harshly, comparing ourselves to others, thinking we could do better. Such judgments are a waste of our time and energy. We are always learning, even if we are sitting on the couch every day thinking we are doing nothing. Each life is useful. A wise soul adds to his resources. The more experience we have, the more we develop our skills, strength, and wisdom. We need a great many varied experiences to develop the wisdom to know what we want and how to create it.

# CHAPTER 12
# SPIRITUAL SURRENDER

We incarnate on planet earth many times. We struggle to survive, feel isolated and abandoned, and face countless challenges before eventually learning how to manage our lives. At last, we believe we control our destiny. How ironic, then, that our final step is surrender.

We can only make the decision to surrender when we feel ready. By surrender, I don't mean waving a white flag. This is a specific type of surrender, the culmination of acquired wisdom. It is really a spiritual surrender.

As we have seen in the early chapters of the book, souls surrender much of their will in their early incarnations. Being incarnated into smaller, closer-knit cultures with more defined social hierarchies is helpful for these young souls as they become used to being on earth. Because they are just at the beginning of the journey, their trust has not yet been broken. When it is, they will commence their journey down the path of separation, thereby generating strength, courage, and knowledge. Through their struggles to reconnect to Source energy, they continue learning, eventually integrating all they have learned into their intuitive wisdom. The stories in the book have shown us how this takes place.

Wise intuition is built upon lifetimes of experience, which we integrate into a deep coherent understanding of our eternal nature and how the earth system works. That doesn't mean we know everything. We are part of a larger self with our own specialties. We decide when we have learned enough to be of value to our larger self. We don't stop learning when we cease incarnating. We are told that expansion is endless, although we may choose periods of rest when we can slow down.

We surrender the power of our egotistical will when we know we can trust ourselves, our inner strength, our courage, and our inner intuitive guidance. The actions we then take are co-creations, a combination of our acquired wisdom and the wise knowledge of our spiritual guides and our larger self.

Does this mean our desires will manifest, that our trust will be rewarded? Perhaps. Spiritual surrender is not a bargain. We don't know what will happen. But we do know, at the deepest level of knowing, that whatever we experience is for the highest good. By its very definition, spiritual surrender means accepting with grace whatever happens.

As we move closer to a state of spiritual surrender, we are tested. Will we retain our trust? In this chapter, we explore cases of souls moving toward this state.

## Sovereignty of the Soul

Surrender includes letting our loved ones be. Usually that means allowing them to resolve their struggles without interfering. We don't like seeing them suffer, but often that is the path they need to take.

Liesel has faced many challenges. In her current life, she has chosen men who were weak in various ways. They were drug dependent, possessive, unemotionally available, or passive aggressive. Her efforts to help them were never successful.

During her first regression, she realized she chose these men because she felt superior, safe, and in control. Because of her fear of rejection, she was self-protective, and her heart was not really open.

In her second regression, Liesel feels an immense tightness around her neck and chest.

*I feel multiple hands on the back of my heart, and that is affecting the energy of my being. They [loving beings] are pushing this energy from my back out through the front of my chest. Now I feel some restriction around my neck. It is so hard to be alone here on the planet. I feel so much emptiness in my chest.*

*Someone said, "Let go!" I am tensely holding onto my chest, trying to protect myself.*

I ask if her guides can help her understand why her chest is so painful.

*I feel so constricted, like I have been wrapped up and dropped in the water. It is cold. I am in a love triangle. I feel betrayed. My lover is not standing by the love he expressed. I am traumatized, shivering and shaking. Really shocked. He is choosing his wife over me. I feel incredibly alone. It feels like I have been stabbed in the heart.*

It turns out she has. Her lover's wife has a knife.

*She stabs me in the left side of my chest. She is saying I am not good enough, that I'm worthless. I am dying, and she stabs me again, this time in the stomach.*

*I am looking into his face. He is shocked that I am going to die. I am realizing that this isn't love. I am going to die around people who do not love me, and I have lost my life because of this. I am young and don't want to die.*

Liesel dies, so shocked and hurt that she becomes stuck and does not return home. Like many other cases in this book, she carried a sense of loss and betrayal into her current life. Although she wanted to avoid feeling like this again, her fears attracted possessive, self-absorbed partners who could not support her emotionally.

In the past life, her lover and his wife bound her up and threw her into cold water.

*I am sinking. Before, I was cold, and now I am warm. I am calm now. I feel like I am floating. Now I feel really light. All of me is relaxed.*

This wasn't the only time Liesel was betrayed. In an earlier life, a wicked person captured her as a young woman and kept her locked up as his possession. Gradually, as she comes to understand how her fears have affected her current relationships, she internalizes an important message.

*I am now feeling love—love for everyone. It is about separating love from possession. Releasing possession from the idea of love takes you to the higher form of love. It is about accepting the sovereignty of the soul.*

Liesel can see how trying to help her partners did not work. It only brought her more suffering. She hadn't realized that attempting to save them was projection. She needed to look inside to save herself, but instead she had externalized this need and expressed it onto others. Her guides point out that surrender means letting go of trying to control the welfare and destiny of people. This is a huge challenge to overcome for those souls who dislike witnessing the suffering of others. But like Liesel and other people in this book, such souls often have some issue in their background (whether in their current life or in a past life) that has not yet been resolved and integrated.

## Creating a Loving Protective Bubble

Learning to create a bubble around us can be useful. During their regressions, several clients have been given the experience of being in a bubble when dealing with difficult people or deaths. Rosaria's case illustrates this well.

Rosaria's guides tell her she is participating in a game. Quite a serious woman, Rosaria starts laughing. She is in a bubble, she tells me, where the game seems funny. We learn she is at the threshold of integrating her human self with her higher self. This bubble shifts her perspective. The bubble is a place to play and remember. She observes that it would be nice to step into it any time.

Earlier in the regression, the guides had suggested it would take time and practice to integrate this higher view of life as a game. We decide to practice, so I remind Rosaria of one of her relatives who doesn't seem to like her. I ask her to imagine hearing this woman's nasty criticisms. Rosaria looks uncomfortable until I ask her to step into the bubble. She laughs immediately.

*It worked. It is hard to be interested in her and why she is so negative when I am in the bubble. It is like stepping into a memory of the game. It makes me laugh.*

Rosario is given the gift of the bubble to help her surrender. The more she meditates and uses the bubble, the easier surrender will become. She will not hook into the petty criticisms of others like she used to. She says she doesn't even need to intellectually know the reasons for their negative behavior. She automatically knows it has nothing to do with her.

Creating a loving protective bubble is easy if you're willing to put in the effort. During meditation, create an image of a bubble surrounding you. Make it transparent, like the bubbles you blow with soap. Perhaps you see or sense the colors of the rainbow in your bubble. Make this bubble as strong as you like, fill it with music or other fun things you enjoy. Now, test it in your imagination. Imagine being near those who frustrate or annoy you. Notice how it feels to emanate light from your bubble while being protected from any external negativity. Watch their negative energy bounce off. Like all imaginative processes, the more we practice this, the stronger our bubble becomes.

# Practicing Surrender

Surrender is difficult to force because we need to be strong and trusting. It comes when we are ready. Once we are at that stage, we know quite clearly that we have a choice. We can continue to act on our fears or surrender our will and follow our guidance.

The guides have pointed out that there is no real surrender unless we already have developed a strong will. Otherwise, we have little to surrender. This reminds me of the popular psychologist Jordan B Peterson, who makes the following suggestion in his lecture on tragedy versus evil: "I don't think that you have any insight whatsoever into your capacity for good until you have some well-developed insight into your capacity for evil."[9]

Souls need to go down a dark path to gain this understanding. Once they know the devastating power of evil and choose its opposite, they are given more responsibility in their lives.

As you become more aware of your true nature as a soul, you have more choice when on the planet. Exercising your free will gives you more freedom, but it also means taking more responsibility.

Some of the people who come to see me have chosen to surrender their will. Our next case, Pearl, is on her way to surrender.

When she came for her session, she met our two very welcoming dogs, each wanting to be in my consulting room. Fortunately, most people who came to see me at that time were animal lovers and didn't mind their presence. My elderly poodle-cross, Harry, was making his bed, as he often did, by noisily scratching the carpet. Stanley, the needy Staffordshire, was loudly trimming his nails with his teeth. I apologized to Pearl, offering to chase

---

9. Jordan B Peterson, "Tragedy vs Evil," March 30, 2013, YouTube video, 42:35, https://www.youtube.com/watch?v=MLp7vWB0TeY&t=25s.

them out of the room. "No problem," she said. "Whatever they are doing is meant to be."

Her past life also demonstrates how far she has come.

In this past life, she is a man, an executive who works for the railways. When an earthquake hits, he is in his office on the other side of the city from his precious family. He tries to reach his wife and two little children, but it is impossible. Fires break out, and a great chasm opens up in the city before he becomes aware of a huge tsunami rolling in. His home is in the suburbs near the sea. He knows it is impossible to save his family, so he heads for higher ground. In those moments, he loses everything he cares about. It is a great shock, and he immediately feels numb.

*It isn't affecting me. I don't feel any emotion.*

But it does affect him, as we discover when I suggest we go to another scene.

*I am in a pub with some friends. I have moved on in time. I have lost my job. I turned to drink, and I am down and out. I can't accept it now. I can't move on. I have lost everything. There is no reason to live. In despair, I can't go on. I am on the edge of a cliff. I see myself jumping. I am at the bottom, broken on the beach. [Cries.] I wasn't even forty. Before the earthquake, everything was going well. What a wasted life!*

Although Pearl thought this was a wasted life, it was not. She soon saw how much she learned from losing everything. In her current life, she lost her beloved husband three years ago. She grieved deeply and vowed she would not succumb to bitterness. She made her mantra: "I am going to fill my life with peace, love, and joy."

Although she has faced many difficulties, she doesn't stress or resist anything. Her beloved mother passed early, and her many family members pose challenges. On the positive side, she is financially self-sufficient. She believes absolutely that everything, every tiny thing, happens for a reason. This is a great comfort to her. She lives with a sense of curiosity and very little fear, accepting whatever happens. This is spiritual surrender.

Trusting, while focusing on the positive, is one way of preparing for surrender.

## Practical Trust

Another client, Lauren, is on this path. She has no stable job, no permanent home, little money, and yet she has total faith that all will be well. Currently, she is living in a supplementary cottage on the property of a generous relative. Even though she had no money for our session when she booked in to see me, by the time of the appointment, she did. Work opportunities seem to appear just when she needs them.

Lauren worked successfully in many roles before she decided to give it all up. For over a decade, she was a policewoman. Later, as a businesswoman, she managed properties worth millions of dollars, but her investment portfolio was heavily leveraged. As she studied spiritual texts, she realized she didn't want to be in debt anymore. It took her years to liquidate all her properties. Then, thanks to the global financial crisis, she ended up with nothing. She didn't care. She was happy being debt-free. Now, she is a free agent, living totally in the present, following her inner guidance, and feeling grateful for each day. She summed up her philosophy:

*I am living with complete knowledge that I am taken care of and will receive what I need. By virtue of my awareness of it, all abundance is available to me.*

She emanates an energy of peace and calm and appears to be living in a state of grace.

Pearl and Lauren are developing the habit of surrender. They believe there is a higher plan and intuitively know all is for the higher good. For some of us, such deep faith is not so easy. Surrendering our will and trusting our deeper guidance can be a challenge.

## Meaning of Surrender

Surrendering comes at the end of your journey. By then, you realize you are in an eternal world, greatly loved, directly connected to Source, and have passed all your major challenges. Surrender means meeting everything with a full and open heart and embracing all learning opportunities, whether pleasant or difficult. Surrendering takes you vibrationally higher and higher.

Surrender is not an easy path. It is a difficult road because you need complete trust. Your trust may be shaken and still recover. If it is broken, you start from scratch. You have to rebuild trust, and that can take time.

Surrendering is constant.

When life is difficult, you have to accept and surrender, trusting your difficulties are ultimately worthwhile. You trust you can handle it and trust it is for the highest good of you and all. This is living faith. It is knowing undoubtedly the truth of your eternal existence.

Constant surrender is the path some souls took in chapter 10, "Avoiding the Depths." This path of trust can be a shortcut to enlightenment because these souls avoid the extremes of separation and perpetration. They came to the earth system after experiencing other dimensions and, while in physical form, were able to keep their connection to Source. Most arrived with little understanding of how the earth system works, but instead of taking a path of deep disconnection to learn, they relied on their spiritual guidance to give them the experiences they needed. Even when they suffered, they managed to retain some level of trust in Source.

Although this is a shorter path to enlightenment, not all souls are able or willing to take it.

In the section "Into the Depths," we learned of souls who chose the long, dark road through extreme separation as coldhearted perpetrators. Once these souls lost their trust in a higher power and cut off their higher-level guidance, they had to rely on trial and error to learn. They descended into difficult lives of victimhood and villainy before finding their way back to the light and redemption. They took the longer path. Each soul chooses the path they take through the earth system. One client, Akali, chose the longer path.

Coming from other planets where she connected strongly with Source, Akali was offered the shorter path to enlightenment. She could retain her spiritual guidance and avoid descending into the darkness. But Akali chose the longer path, believing it would help her gain clarity and a deep understanding of humanity. This matters to Akali, for she is a healer soul. As she emerges from the darkness, she will be better able to help those who are lost.

*I have a strong, ongoing desire to help people. I have come a long way on a long journey. I have come with an understanding of what it's like to struggle, but that compassion is instilled from that long journey.*

*I was asked to surrender years ago, but I like to analyze things. I like to ask questions. My guide is smiling at me. He knows I am an eager soul. He thinks I am stubborn. If I could accept what is given to me, just let go and go along and learn the lessons ... I guess I've been doing it the hard way. I will still get there.*

I ask if there are any advantages to taking the longer path.

*Doing it the hard way increases the capacity of your soul to a vast extent. The soul expands more, and its energy grows larger. You have* more to give. *The ones who are taking the longer path, we're helping others as well as helping ourselves.*

Those, like Akali, who eventually transcend the dark path, develop a charisma that makes them relatable to other souls who are still deeply lost. These transcendent souls are now able to help the lost ones awaken. Even though this is a longer path, those wishing to help deeply lost souls find it worthwhile.

## The Call to Closer Connection

I have noticed that some clients are highly motivated. In previous lives they took it easy, making little progress. Now they are keen to make up for lost time and really "show up," words used by Brené Brown to describe stepping out of our comfort zone.[10] Brené Brown, professor at the University of Houston, has conducted research into "courage, vulnerability, shame, and empathy."[11] She has found we grow courage by embracing our vulnerability and taking on challenges.

Some of my clients feel they are called to progress and grow. One is Belinda. During her regression, she identifies a problem.

*I do feel in the last twelve months that I am working toward something, but something else is getting in the way. Those in my soul family want me to stop progressing because I could go to another realm.*

*I am being held back because others are being left behind, and it is important that others are not left behind because of our connection. We have ancestral lines on earth, and it is also like that with our souls. But some are choosing not to progress.*

---

10. Brené Brown, *Brené Brown: The Call to Courage,* documentary film, directed by Sandra Restrepo, Netflix, 76 min., 2019.
11. "Brené Brown," University of Houston Graduate College of Social Work, accessed July 2, 2021, https://www.uh.edu/socialwork/about/faculty-directory/b-brown/.

I ask what could happen if they refuse to progress.

*There could be a separation. They would be on another level. I wouldn't like that, but I feel a need to progress. The guides tell me that sustaining a higher level of frequency and reaching a critical mass has the potential to pull them up.*

In her life between lives, Belinda meets with her soul group. She asks to see her mother, who has passed.

*My mother is right here. She is not liking what we are talking about because she is one of the ones who don't want to progress. Her family are on the same level, caught in circles of negativity. She says I should be happy where I am.*

*This is a time when there is a lot of change, and some souls will progress and some won't. There will be a division. I feel a little bit of sadness.*

Belinda knows she will continue progressing by working with others in her soul group to create the magnetic frequencies needed to pull the other souls up. Her soul group needs to be ready when it is time to move on to new experiences.

## Time to Go

The current era on earth is one of those times when progression is easier than earlier periods. Those souls who are close to having a sufficient level of development are being offered opportunities to complete their curriculum in the earth school. If they accept the offer, they will receive experiences needed to balance and release any leftover issues. If they ask for it, they will receive helpful advice, which, if followed, will aid their progress. Some clients refer to this process as graduation, although they are told coming back or not is always their choice.

Graduating from the earth school is similar in some ways to graduating from university. You can remain at university and teach others, or you might leave and find careers that utilize what you have learned. While graduation means you have completed the curriculum and no longer need to return to earth, there is always more you can learn.

I've had a few clients who have reached this level of development. One is Graham, an engineer who has travelled, worked in various countries, married twice, had children, overcome many challenges, and created a loving happy life. Graham doesn't need to incarnate anymore. He also has terminal cancer.

When Graham came to see me, he said he was calm and well. He looked well too. I thought we might be able to clear his issues so he could live a longer life. After meeting his soul group, he asked why he has cancer. He was given a definitive answer:

*"You have done what you were supposed to do in this life and succeeded."* [Long pause.] *I feel sad that it is coming to an end.*

I felt compelled to ask what job he would be doing on the other side.

*I need to help people when they incarnate. I just heard, "You are going to be a guide."*

Feeling cheerful, I blurted out a response, "Oh! That's a great job!"

Graham wept gently. Then he replied, his voice humble, *They are very proud of me.*

Being in touch with both his human self and his larger self, Graham expressed how he felt.

*I am crying here but not over there. There, I am happy.*

Although Graham doesn't need to incarnate again, he may. Guides come back occasionally for a short stint to remember what it is like being human.

One quality Graham shares with the guides is respect for free will and the sovereignty of the soul. Guides do not interfere with the intentions of their clients unless given explicit permission. They watch compassionately while allowing their charges to learn through confusion, mistakes, and dead-end turns. I recall many of my clients being advised to practice this high level of respect for people and their soul journeys.

## Conclusion

Spiritual surrender is a decisive step on our path forward. Surrendering means letting go of the need to control, instead having complete trust in our ability to lovingly accept ourselves, others, and all that is happening. It is trust in Source and the greater plan for planet earth.

We on earth are facing many challenges. I have a sense there will be many openings for those like Graham who are at the point of surrender and ready to take on the job of being a guide. These are souls who have been lost, found their way back, and completed their challenges.

Perhaps you already know you are one of these souls who have been called to move forward. Maybe, as you read this chapter, you suddenly got goosebumps. Perhaps an image flashed through your mind, or you felt a twinge or an inkling that you are one of those being invited. If so, you need to decide if you want to take this opportunity to progress quickly in the earth system. There is still time. Even if you have other lifetimes to complete, you can speed up your spiritual evolution by practicing surrender. You can do this by listening to your inner guidance, reflecting on it, acting on it if it makes sense to you, and then accepting whatever comes your way.

At a higher level, there is no "good" or "bad." Every action or event is important for moving forward. Challenging circumstances are nothing more than opportunities to learn and grow—as we have discovered with the many cases in this book.

You can ask your guides to present appropriate learning opportunities to you, and then ask for their help and guidance as you take them on. Having confidence in your guides, yourself, and the larger system is paramount. Developing robust trust is an essential element during our destined journey toward spiritual surrender.

# CONCLUSION

Earth is an amazing place, and just as spectacular are the billions of souls brave enough to come here to experience it. In this book, we have explored many cases, learning how difficult and challenging, as well as powerful and uplifting, our lives can be.

It is not all darkness and pain. Being human is exhilarating and noble, multifaceted and rich. Human life is a gift. Each life is valuable and necessary.

We can be too hard on ourselves, expecting so much, feeling worthless and self-critical. From the stories in this book, I hope each of you begins shifting any critical view you've held, congratulating yourself for undertaking your earthly journey. The guides have told us many times that just being on the planet in a human body is courageous and admirable—no matter how we play out our lives.

We are all brave souls with inner strength and resources. Many of us need to focus on what we have achieved over our current life and many lifetimes. We have overcome many challenges and are still here, taking on more. Once we understand how challenging this journey really is, we become less judgmental of ourselves and others.

We have seen that those who build walls are trembling like jelly on the inside. Feeling abandoned and terrified of love, the only path they perceive is putting up walls of protection. The more isolated they feel, the more they reinforce their walls, creating a vicious circle that is not easily broken. Of course, this is an important part of our earthly journey. Although not all souls choose to be perpetrators, we need to experience enough isolation to understand those who do.

The naïve mind sees strength in those who are controlling, forceful, or violent. Many fear such people. But we have seen that those using force and intimidation are empty on the inside, playing out cruel games in an attempt to repress their deep feelings of shame.

From the journeys of the clients in this book, we have learned that our lives are planned to various degrees, and yet we have free will while executing our plan. We have learned that souls cannot easily choose to be abusive in one life and compassionate in the next. These cases demonstrate the long, debilitating struggle many souls endure before emerging into light after their dark night of the soul. Souls evolve slowly over many incarnations, just as humans gradually evolve during the many experiences of one lifetime.

Being victimized for our naivety is another part of the journey. How do we really understand others without matching their experience? This is an experiential planet. We learn through experience.

We saw that true strength comes from the inside. To deepen our connection to others, we must allow ourselves to be vulnerable. The walls need to come down. To be vulnerable, we need a strong core, a deep knowledge of our inner strength, our integrity, and our immortality. To open up emotionally, we need to focus on the challenges we have overcome. As children, we had one primary job: to get to adulthood. All of us experienced challenges. Some of us had to deal with bullies, broken families, mean people, neglect, or abuse. Whatever we experienced, becoming an adult is a great achievement. How many of us acknowledge our child self for this accomplishment? We easily recall our shortcomings, but how often do we focus on our insights, our sincere efforts, our good deeds, and our humble successes?

Consciously making the choice to soften and open our heart, even when we don't know how to do it, is a step that begins the process. Practicing meditation, surfacing and accepting our fears, while asking for help to release them, will eventually calm our mind. When we truly desire to connect and are willing to be vulnerable, our spiritual guides will help. We will meet situations designed to open our hearts. Our courage will grow as we face our challenges rather than finding distractions.

Yearning to know how to grow spiritually means we are on the path of developing our intuition, knowledge, and wisdom. No matter how tough life may feel at times, we are progressing and will emerge into love and light.

Our intuition is guidance from Source, manifesting through our mind and body. Intuition is the most valuable faculty we have because wise intuition is built on integrated experience, giving us wisdom and spiritual truth. Once we are truly connected to our higher guidance, there is nothing to fear. We are on the road to completing our life's purpose.

We have seen how the present is a culmination of the past. Past life trauma can still be active and affect our current lives. Some undertake a regression to surface any leftover issues interfering with their spiritual progress, but there are many ways to address current concerns.

One way to proceed is asking for guidance while trusting that help will come. Listening, being open to signals, hunches, and nudges is important. Expecting to be guided to the next step and being brave enough to take it places us squarely on our path. Clearing up trauma from our past lives or current life is tremendously liberating.

Being at a stage where any leftover fears can be released means we can practice surrender and live a peaceful, loving, and joyful life. Joy is important. Joy spreads. Pure joy has a sense of calmness in it, a sweet, gentle joy. It is like a simple smile radiating a special beauty, a wise stillness and deep acceptance.

When you are rich with a wealth of experience, you own a treasure chest filled with jewels of many colors and facets. Some are perfect, while others may be flawed or cloudy. When you meet another, you reach into your treasure chest and intuitively pick up the exact jewel reflecting the same facets of experience and understanding, allowing you to touch the other. This is trusting you have all that you need. "Being" rather than striving. The transfer is energetic, happening on a completely different dimensional level, imparting the knowledge that is desired and needed by the other.

The cloudiness in the jewels is unresolved emotions. Each of us has the responsibility to release these. Although they played a useful role in our development, they are no longer needed. Eventually, we don't see the clouds anymore, just clarity. Now we are able to hold positive and nurturing energy for the other. In the beginning there is the raw stone, the diamond in the rough, and then comes the honing and the clearing up. The emotional cloudiness is released. The cutting and honing come from our experience, and then we reflect and make connections, putting it all together. That is our path: becoming clear, light, and wise, reflecting love, joy, and peace.

For nearly thirty years, I have been helping clients with their emotional issues. I noticed when I cleared an issue in my own life, I would immediately attract clients who were grappling with similar problems. Even to this day, I notice the same pattern. Clients follow close in the wake of my own healing.

Resolving our issues allows us to resonate with those who are wrestling with the same challenges. This resonance doesn't just apply to adversities in our current life; it applies to our past lives too. This is why so many healer souls choose to have lives as perpetrators and lives as victims. The deeper their experience, once resolved and integrated, the greater their ability to assist others.

As the shame researcher Brené Brown has said: "Only when we are brave enough to explore the darkness will we discover the infinite power of our light."[12]

Our calling is to trust, knowing the greater plan playing out is as brilliant and beautiful as the planet on which we live.

The dark night of souls is part of this plan. We cannot see in the dark unless we shine a light on the darkness. Truth can free us. Knowledge expands us, and wisdom brings peace and fulfillment. We cannot appreciate the warmth of the sun unless we have felt the cold of the night.

My hope is that each of us can shine a light on our darkest experiences and bring more joy, love, and gratitude into our lives and into our world.

---

12. Brené Brown, *Daring Greatly: How the Courage to Be Vulnerable Transforms the Way We Live, Love, Parent, and Lead* (UK: Penguin Life, 2015), 60.

# RECOMMENDED RESOURCES

Brown, Brené. *Daring Greatly: How the Courage to Be Vulnerable Trans-forms the Way We Live, Love, Parent, and Lead*. UK: Penguin Life, 2015. A useful book exploring the importance of vulnerability—a quality we all need to develop on our spiritual journeys.

Clark, Ann J. *Healing from Great Loss: Facing Pain and Grief to Recover Your Authentic Self*. Woodbury, MN: Llewellyn Worldwide, 2021. In this book, Dr. Clark, a Michael Newton Institute practitioner, shares many stories, including her own, about experiencing profound grief from a significant loss, whether it be through death, divorce, a health crisis, career disruption, or financial ruin. These powerful stories include a spiritual perspective and show us how healing is possible through a connection with our inner guidance, allowing us to gain a deeper understanding of the reasons behind the loss.

Clark, Ann J., Karen Joy, Joanne Selinske, and Marilyn Hargreaves. *Wisdom of Souls: Case Studies of Life Between Lives from the Michael Newton Institute*. Woodbury, MN: Llewellyn Publications, 2019. This book includes cases from over twenty practitioners of the Newton Institute focused on common issues we all face in life.

Clark, Ann J., Karen Joy, Marilyn Hargreaves, and Joanne Selinske. *Llewellyn's Little Book of Life Between Lives*. Woodbury, MN: Llewellyn Publications, 2019. Michael Newton asked the members of the Michael Newton Institute Research Committee to write this book, which summarized the process of the hypnotic regressions that made him famous. It contains information on past life and life between lives regressions using illustrative cases provided by the four practitioner authors.

Department of Perceptual Studies, University of Virginia website has a number of informative videos for those who are looking for evidence of life after death. https://med.virginia.edu/perceptual -studies/dops-media/selected-videos-dops-research-overview/.

*Exploring Past Lives with Karen Joy* (podcast). In this podcast, Karen interviews people who have relived their past lives and/or visited their life between lives. These people come from all walks of life, with many different issues. Listeners discover why Karen's guests wanted to undertake a regression in the first place, how each past life is unique, what it was like re-living a past life, the relationship between their past life and current life and the impact of the experience on their life, their personal relationships and future. https:// lifebetweenlivesregression.com.au/podcasts/.

Insight Timer Meditation App. https://insighttimer.com. This free app has over 100,000 meditations. There is also a member plus option, which unlocks more features, and you can also donate. It is an amazing resource with many courses and talks (e.g., yoga and mindfulness) as well as meditations for sleep, morning energy, anxiety, and stress. I use it most days.

Joy, Karen. *Other Lives, Other Realms: Journeys of Transformation.* 2nd ed. Maleny, Queensland: MediaLuna, 2019. My first book on spiritual hypnosis. I explore the nature and benefits of past life and life between lives regressions.

Life Between Lives Regression (my website): https://lifebetween livesregression.com.au. Sign up to receive my regular blog, my podcast, and other resources, including a guided meditation. You can also follow me at KarenJoyAuthor on Twitter, Instagram, and Facebook.

Newton, Michael. *Destiny of Souls: New Case Studies of Life Between Lives*. St. Paul, MN: Llewellyn Publications, 2000. The second book by Dr. Newton provides more information about our life between lives and includes helpful, informative cases.

———. *Journey of Souls: Case Studies of Life Between Lives*. St. Paul, MN: Llewellyn Publications, 1994. The first book by Dr. Newton explores in some detail the place we call our life between lives, with excerpts from his sessions with clients.

Selinske, Joanne, *Awakened Soul: Discoveries of Healing, Self-Love and Spiritual Growth*. Baltimore: Amare Press, 2021. The path to wholeness is littered with emotional impediments. *Awakened Soul* shows us how spiritual regression can help remedy our obstacles while fostering self-love and awakening.

# BIBLIOGRAPHY

Brown, Brené. *Brené Brown: The Call to Courage.* Documentary film. Directed by Sandra Restrepo. Netflix, 76 min., 2019.

"Dark Energy, Dark Matter." What We Study. NASA. Accessed April 29, 2021. https://science.nasa.gov/astrophysics/focus-areas/what-is-dark-energy.

Keeton, Charles, and Arlie Petters. "Tiny Black Holes." NOVA. October 30, 2006. https://www.pbs.org/wgbh/nova/article/tiny-black-holes/.

Newton, Michael. *Destiny of Souls: New Case Studies of Life Between Lives.* St. Paul, MN: Llewellyn Publications, 2000.

———. *Journey of Souls: Case Studies of Life Between Lives.* St. Paul, MN: Llewellyn Publications, 2004.

Peterson, Jordan B, "Tragedy vs Evil." March 30, 2013. YouTube video, 42:35, https://www.youtube.com/watch?v=MLp7vWB0TeY&t=25s.

"UVA Medical Center Hour: Is There Life after Death? 50 Years of Research at UVA DOPS, 2017." University of Virginia, Division of Perceptual Studies. February 22, 2017. https://med.virginia.edu/perceptual-studies/dops-media/selected-videos-dops-research-overview/.

## To Write to the Author

If you wish to contact the author or would like more information about this book, please write to the author in care of Llewellyn Worldwide Ltd. and we will forward your request. Both the author and publisher appreciate hearing from you and learning of your enjoyment of this book and how it has helped you. Llewellyn Worldwide Ltd. cannot guarantee that every letter written to the author can be answered, but all will be forwarded. Please write to:

Karen Joy
℅ Llewellyn Worldwide
2143 Wooddale Drive
Woodbury, MN 55125-2989
Please enclose a self-addressed stamped envelope for reply,
or $1.00 to cover costs. If outside the U.S.A., enclose
an international postal reply coupon.

Many of Llewellyn's authors have websites with additional information and resources. For more information, please visit our website at http://www.llewellyn.com